LAMBDA

λ

GRAY

LAMBDA

Jeanne Adleman

R. Berger

Malcolm Boyd

Vashte Doublex

Marcia Freedman

William S. Hubbard

Morris Kight

Arlene Kochman

Mina K. Robinson Meyer

Sharon M. Raphael

A PRACTICAL, EMOTIONAL, AND SPIRITUAL GUIDE FOR GAYS AND LESBIANS WHO ARE GROWING OLDER

GRAY

NEWCASTLE PUBLISHING, NORTH HOLLYWOOD, CALIFORNIA

Conceived and compiled by Karen Westerberg Reyes
Edited by Lorena Fletcher Farrell
Copy edited by Gina Renée Gross
Cover and interior design by Michele Lanci-Altomare

ISBN: 0-87877-179-4
A Newcastle Book
First printing, 1993
10 9 8 7 6 5 4 3 2 1
Printed in the United States of America.

DEDICATIONS

With all my love to Dan,
who introduced me to the
extraordinary men and women
of Van Ness Recovery House,
and to his life partner, Steve,
who is truly a very lucky man.

—Karen Westerberg Reyes

For my adored James and dear David.
Together they will *win the war.*

—Lorena Fletcher Farrell

λ

CONTENTS

Jeanne Adleman relates her own personal triumphs after deciding, at the age of sixty, to live the rest of her life as a lesbian. "Some of the questions I had to deal with were inside my skin and within my brain. Who would I tell, and why and when and how? I have always disliked the phrase 'coming out.' I recognize now that it is a kind of shorthand for a series of steps one probably must take to fully embrace a lesbian or gay life, whether or not one has previously been hiding in some 'closet.' "

R. Berger communicates his feelings and philosophies on growing older. "While some of my perspectives have changed, I'm essentially the same person I always was. I've had a few hardships along the way (gotten ill, lost loved ones to AIDS, ended unhappy relationships), but maybe I survived *because* I continued to be the same person. The single constant denominator has been my identity, my sense of self. This is who I am, nothing has ever changed that, and nothing will—so perhaps I'll get through this life after all."

Malcolm Boyd shares his remarkable outlook on life. "Most of my life I avoided the sacredness, wonder, and pleasure of the moment. I was restless and in a hurry to get beyond the present to the next place, the enticing future. This is true no longer. Finally I comprehend the sense of a famous ad for a steamship line: Getting there is half the fun. Half the meaning. So, it's the journey that occupies me now. The journey that offers those tantalizing forks in the road. The journey that is in the present."

Vashte Doublex explores her own struggle with the excitements and fears of liberation. "The women's movement and lesbian feminism have opened my eyes, my mind, my spirit, giving me pride in myself and in other women, allowing me to see what miracles we perform daily. I have come to appreciate our struggles and differences, even the separations and probable reconciliations."

Marcia Freedman reveals how she came to terms with aging as she watched her mother's final years. "Until her last day, when she walked with great difficulty and could maintain an activity only for an hour or so without tiring, she was a ball of hot energy that filled all the space available to her. I watched all she did and was with amazement and admiration. I learned from her during those years that the physical body would be what it is, but the spirit could be anything one wished."

CHAPTER 6 — page 77
MORRIS KIGHT
Will You Still Love Me When I'm Seventy-Four?

Morris Kight recounts the events of the rebellion. "In 1969, spurred on by the anti-war movement, black power movement, and the hippie revolution, we found it in our best interest to commence a nonviolent revolution. Thus in late 1969 Gay Liberation fronts were created in New York, Berkeley, Los Angeles, San Francisco, and San Jose, California, in that order. During 1970 very nearly three hundred sprang up in the country, and the world has been a far better place for us ever since."

CHAPTER 7 — page 93
ARLENE KOCHMAN
Old and Gay

Arlene Kochman outlines where older gays and lesbians are coming from. "The choice of invisibility should not be scoffed at by the younger activist members of the gay and lesbian community; it should be understood in the context of our history and experience in this society. Our invisibility is related to fear, which is based on past and present societal prejudices. Though the gay and lesbian community has come a long way concerning civil rights, living with and often internalizing constant homophobia is difficult to overcome."

Sharon M. Raphael and Mina K. Robinson Meyer relate the old lesbians' movement to its social ramifications. "We have had the unique opportunity to witness and observe the genesis of a new social movement. This movement, which is still giving birth to itself, is one we would broadly define as a movement to empower old lesbians. We wish to share some of our experiences and insights with the hope that the reader will learn that no one is too old to speak out for herself and her rights, transforming her world."

Gail J. Koff discusses the slow—but, it is hoped, sure—liberalization of both laws and legal interpretations regarding gay rights. "This growing public awareness has also had an impact on the law, which is undergoing an upheaval in an attempt to deal with the changes occurring in the social arena. Cases now reaching the court system promise to have a long-lasting effect on how gay men and lesbians are treated under the law. Further complicating the situation, however, is the fact that in many areas homosexuals are not only considered social pariahs but are also subject to archaic laws that have been on the books for a century or more that make their sexual practices illegal."

William S. Hubbard compiles one of the most complete resource lists of information for gay and lesbian persons.

"Knowledge concerning men's and women's journeys across gay and lesbian life courses has been marginalized within gerontology. This annotated resource chapter is intended as a tool of empowerment that educators, practitioners, and researchers can use in their personal and professional lives as they move gay and lesbian issues into the gerontological mainstream."

FOREWORD

BY MARK THOMPSON
senior editor, *The Advocate*

One of the things that scared me most as a young gay man was the stereotypical image of the older homosexual: predatory, pitiful, a lonely outcast even among his or her own kind. Once the flush of youth had passed, such was the twilight fate certain to befall those who strayed from the straight and narrow. Just thinking about it made me shudder. Coming out to a life that would end so sadly seemed all the better reason to stay in the closet.

But now, after having happily lived through two decades as an openly gay man, I can see what a lie those early notions were. With my twenties and thirties behind me, I stand looking expectantly into middle age and beyond. The view is not dim, but is lit with promise and real anticipation of wonder to come. The gloomy picture of being senior and gay that once caused me so much doubt—as it has so many others—I now understand as a double-edged myth society uses to intimidate those who dare to claim their difference.

Most boldly, this myth asserts that to be gay or lesbian is simply wrong. Just as negatively, but more covertly, it tells us that if you must lead a homosexual lifestyle, get it over with as soon as possible—the world just doesn't have room for older queers. This intolerant message cuts deep into the hearts and minds of all gay people, no matter how young or old. The myth is homophobia's prime instrument, an insidious decree that has provoked more than forty years of brave, organized resistance from the individuals it would ban.

With important books like *Lambda Gray* in hand, I think our task is made a little easier. We've all grown in self-acceptance. Concurrent with that awareness has been insight about the special qualities of being gay or lesbian. We're pioneer people, for one thing—survivors who've forged durable lives out of a relatively unexplored and hostile frontier. This has resulted in resourceful, creative imaginations, all the better equipped to deal with life's ever-changing scenario, including its old age.

Because we're adept at creating close-knit communities, both intimate and large, gay men and lesbians are also better prepared to wage the political battles necessary for maintaining quality of life. These are lessons all Americans need to learn; not just the aging majority Baby Boom generation but everyone— especially as life becomes increasingly complex and pluralistic. In other words, gay people can set powerful examples not only about establishing a life to call their own, but about sustaining that life year after year into ripe older age.

Of course, to disseminate our discoveries we must first believe we have something authentic to share. And that is where the writers of this book come in. The voice of gay and lesbian seniors has seldom been heard, even within their own community. That silence can be attributed as much to society's homophobia as to its reluctance to deal with growing older. We all, whether gay or straight, live in a culture obsessed with youth and beauty. Fortunately, that blind sight is at last being liberated. The authors here are making a path of understanding anyone can gain from, for they are being nothing less than completely human.

With so much to learn, there is no time to fear—even less time to doubt—any amount of wisdom. And here, in the experienced words of those who have lived fully and, yes, gaily, can be found pathways to hopeful places.

PREFACE

BY KAREN WESTERBERG REYES

Lambda Gray was conceived out of love, respect, acknowledgement, and some concern for one of the most vital—and ignored—groups in existence: older gays and lesbians. The birth of this book is a story in itself. A story of coincidences and dead ends, happenstances and chance meetings. All the while I was working on it I felt that it was guiding its own creation. Frustration would turn into revelation, rejection into opportunity, misuderstanding into purpose.

Lambda Gray started with a question; my question, spoken within the context of gerontological studies at the University of Southern California. There must be, I thought, a group of older people, unacknowledged, unappreciated, and unaccomodated, who could benefit from some academic attention. I loathed the prospect of expending my energies on some esoteric aspect of institutional abstruseness. I give all due respect to those academicians who spend their lives searching out and studying minutiae. I'm sure our world is the better for it. I'm just as sure that path is not for me.

Enter now a cast of characters and locations as diverse as the universe.

DAN AND STEVE

I first met Dan Robertson in Palm Springs, California, basking (or I should say baking, thanks to his red hair and fair complexion) by the pool. My husband, Vince, and I had just purchased a vacation condominium to celebrate the fact that we had propelled ourselves, after almost twenty years of hard work, into a tax bracket that allowed such luxuries. It was a completely new realm for us and we walked carefully. We didn't want to stand out as the new kids on the block in this small spalsh of semi-prosperity.

Dan and his life partner, Steve Schulo, were almost founding fathers of the condominium complex, having bought their weekend retreat years earlier. They offered a friendship of the kind and quality I had seldom experienced: genuine, supportive, undemanding, funny, sincere, free, outrageous, and boundless. Vince and I (sometimes together, sometimes separately) went on a glorious ride with them—to restaurants, clubs, galleries, holes-in-the-wall, museums, shopping centers, movie houses, and on tours (which they guided) in, around, through, and beside the expanses of Palm Springs. Dan and Steve made us natives in many easy-to-take lessons. And they taught us how to have fun again, something we had forgotten during those years of striving and raising three children.

They introduced us to their friends, a wonderful conglomeration of intellectuals, relatives, vamps, and vagabonds they had collected over the years. They stuffed a different combination of these amazing people into the spare spaces of their condo almost every weekend. And I realized, over time, that these people were much more than friends to Dan and Steve. They were family (as Vince and I had become). And thus I had my first lesson in community.

THE PARAMOUNT REVELATION

Move now to a balmy evening on the grounds of Paramount Studios in Hollywood. The event: a fundraiser for The Van Ness Recovery House, one of the very few places of recovery from alcoholism for gay men and lesbians in this part of California. Dan, a recovering alcoholic, gives much time and attention to the House where, he says, he found his salvation and entrance back into life after a many-year affair with booze.

It is a glorious evening. Throngs of people pour through the gates to a festively decorated expanse of buildings and booths. Dress is semi-formal; tuxedos and gowns of every hue and cut. A Monte Carlo atmosphere is apparent despite the fact that the money being wagered on the bright games of roulette and blackjack is scrip. The dealers and croupiers come from the tables of Las Vegas and have donated their time. When all the elements are put together, the event becomes more than the sum of its parts, more than an avenue for raising money. It is a sensation, a feast, a swell of what appears to be, on the surface, happy humanity orchestrated by laughter, friendly talk and shouts.

But then I look closer.

The crowds of mostly gay men seem to be undergoing a sort of self-administered segregation as the night wears on. The young steep themselves in a boastful, energetic, and vociferous haze in contrast to the older men, who exude an aura of reticence and almost-apology. I see this dichotomy in almost every corner, surging beneath a layer of glittering camaraderie. I see an almost palpable surge of alienation manifested in glance and body language between the younger and older groups. This phenomenon isn't total, but it is widespread enough for me to notice. And it makes me wonder.

From this glance, this glimpse into something I'm not even sure is really there, comes an idea.

MEETING MR. BERGER

I talk to Dan and Steve about my observations. Am I seeing ghosts? Reading something into the situation that does not exist? No, they assure. There is an invisible but very real barrier between young and old gay men. It's a mixture of fear, dread, and misunderstanding. The young, so openly gay and obstinate, don't understand their older brothers who remain (or remained so long) in the security of the closet. The young shout gay pride, wear it like a banner, pick it up like a flag, and wave it in the face of society. They move forward and can't understand the quiet desperation of some of their elders.

Dan loaned me his copy of *Gay and Gray* by Ray Berger. And I began to understand. At the same time I knew I could never *fully* understand. That would be presumptuous. As I talked to people about my book idea, looked for someone to compile it, I worried about this. Would I come off as some sanctimonious do-gooder in my work in this area? Who did I think I was? As time went on, I decided that my point of heterosexual non-reference, so to speak, might be a benefit more than a detriment. It gave me a field of objectivity. I could remain an observer. Maybe, I thought, I could understand enough to gather a study of some sort, a compilation of the strongest and wisest gay and lesbian voices. But where would I find those voices?

I met Ray Berger in his office at California State University, Long Beach. I told him about my search for someone to shepherd such a book. I explained how I had come to take on this mantle. I told him of the publisher, Al Saunders, who wanted and believed in the book. It was a done deal, I explained to him. He wouldn't have to look for a publisher, go through that angst. All he had to do was deliver, and we would be there ready to take the finished product and print it. What could be easier? We talked about many things, and one of them was his illness. He was too busy and, at times, too ill to even think about taking on such an endeavor. But he gave me names. And lists of other books to read. And we talked. And I learned a little more.

Throughout the gathering and editing process of *Lambda Gray*, Ray has been an invaluable counselor. He agreed to be a contributor, finally, after some coaxing. How could this book appear without his imprimatur on it somewhere, I asked? After all, he was the first one to look into the phenomenon of older gay men, their special problems, fears, and challenges.

THE AMERICAN SOCIETY ON AGING CONNECTION

My work as an editor at *Modern Maturity* magazine takes me to many gerontological conferences. At this particular confab I noticed that a workshop on gay and lesbian aging was scheduled one evening. I decided to attend.

It was at this meeting that I met the movers and shakers in the field of gay and lesbian aging. I was surprised, and somewhat humbled. I didn't realize its forces were so organized, so strong. The group members were, to a person, dedicated to studying the particular problems of older gays and lesbians. I talked to Sharon Raphael and Mina Meyer that night. I told them, and the group, about my book. They were receptive. But I could see they were also a bit puzzled. Who was I? What was I doing this for? Time, much discussion, and another year would convince them that my intentions were honorable.

It was at a later ASA conference on "Diversity with a Difference" in San Francisco that I learned more about another phenomenon—the invisibility of older lesbians. I would make sure they weren't invisible in my book.

I was still learning. But I had enough to start. I had a direction and I had, at last, found *Lambda Gray*'s voices. May their messages ring loud and clear. May their counsel help and guide.

LAMBDA

—— λ ——

GRAY

CHAPTER 1

To Find a Place

BY
JEANNE ADLEMAN

About the Author: Born in 1919, Jeanne Adleman spent fifty-three years in and around New York City before moving to San Francisco in 1972. Like many others during the Great Depression, she went to work young, to college at night, and then dropped out. Returning to school much later, she earned her B.A. in education (with departmental honors) at the age of forty-one. Two years later she was invited back to teach in that department.

After some further delays she earned an M.A. in teacher education at Columbia University Teachers College. Eventually she taught at other colleges, but never with tenure. At sixty-two she enrolled in a doctoral program in psychology, then withdrew after two years because of both rising costs and philosophical differences.

An educator-turned-feminist-therapist, Adleman has a consulting practice in San Francisco. She is the author of "Falling and Rising in Love" in the collection *Long Time Passing: Lives of Older Lesbians* (Alyson, 1986). The chapter appears, reprinted, in *The Welcoming Congregation: Resources for Affirming Gay, Lesbian, and Bisexual Persons* (Unitarian Universalist Association, 1990). Jeanne Adleman is writing a book on choosing at midlife or later to become a lesbian, and has also had writing published in *Broomstick*, a magazine by, for, and about women over forty.

Her professional writings include "Necessary Risks and Ethical Constraints" in *Feminist Ethics in Psychology* (Springer, 1990). Currently she is co-editing a book provisionally titled *Racism in the Lives of Women: Testimony, Theory, and Guides to Practice*, to be published by The Haworth Press. Locally, Adleman is a member of the advisory board of Gay and Lesbian Outreach to Elders (GLOE) and a former board member of The Women's Building of the Bay Area. Nationally, she served for seven years, two of them as chairperson, on the Steering Committee of the Feminist Therapy Institute, Inc.

λ

"Die early or get old. There is no other alternative." Stark words by Simone de Beauvoir at the opening of Part II of her comprehensive book, *Coming of Age.*

Reading them took my breath away. They revealed a truth I should have known but had not consciously considered before. In my fifties, therefore, I decided I would chose to die early. Better to end with a bang than a whimper, I thought.

I am seventy-three as I write this essay, and I have changed my mind. But I am not sure I would have changed my mind had I not decided at sixty to live the rest of my life as a lesbian. Did I know all of what this would mean? No, though I thought I did. I had many illusions about what lesbian life would be.

Some of the questions I did not deal with until after my decision were external. What *is* a lesbian, really? Who are the real lesbians? Who decides? A woman professional some years older than I, known to me and only a few others as a lesbian, asked, "How can a woman spend years married to a man, apparently finding heterosexuality agreeable, then suddenly change?" Then she answered herself, "She must have been a lesbian all along, but denying it to herself."

Many lesbians I have interviewed or otherwise met, who at forty-five or after made decisions like mine, phrase this as "before I recognized my lesbianism." For them, as for my friend, lesbianism is something inborn. Others say, "I fell in love with a woman and found what I'd been looking for without knowing it."

For myself and many others who love women, having had intense intimate friendships and comradely alliances with women, even having been sexually aroused by a certain woman, didn't bring up images of ourselves as lesbians because our primary sexual affiliations were with men. For us it was the women's liberation movement, which challenged most or all of our heterosexual assumptions, that made such a life change possible.

Some of the questions I now had to deal with were inside my skin and within my brain. Who would I tell, and why, and when and how? I have always disliked the phrase "coming out." I recognize now that it is a kind of shorthand for a series of steps one probably must take to fully embrace a lesbian or gay life, whether or not one has previously been hiding in some "closet."

Personally, my first felt need was to communicate my determination—to live the rest of my life as a lesbian—to my immediate family, and to do it fast enough that each would hear it directly from me. For some years I had been referring to myself as an ex-mother. I didn't mean that I wanted to disconnect from the people who knew me as mother or stepmother; I meant that I wanted to drop the role of mother. The children had, after all, grown up. They were adults. I seemed unable to refer to them as my "children." I wanted their expectations of me to change, our relationships to become egalitarian.

Perhaps this is why I never wanted them to live with me again, any more than I wanted my mother to live with me or wanted to live with her or with them. By the time I was sixty these formerly children were ages thirty to forty. I love them all, have loved them through their own innumerable changes, and do not want to grow even older than I am living by myself. Even less do I want to live with any of them or expect them to take care of me financially.

One daughter's response was, "Well, what can I say? You're not a kid. I hope you know what you're doing. I hope you'll be happy." Another daughter said, "Just remember that you don't know what heartbreak is until your heart has been broken by a woman."

Only my son asked questions. First he asked if I had forgotten that he had two lesbian sisters. Oddly enough, in preparing to tell him my big news, I had forgotten that one of his sisters had for four years considered herself "a lesbian at that time," and that another was still a declared lesbian. "I did forget," I told him, "but I do think it's different when it's your mother."

A bit later the same evening he asked, "What does being a lesbian mean to you, Mother?" It was a most reasonable question, but I had not anticipated it. I gave him a hasty answer then asked what had been behind his question. He had heard some not entirely inaccurate stories, when his sister was deciding she wasn't a lesbian after all, about lesbians who wanted to kill all boy babies, for example, and about lesbians who refused to have anything to do with men or boys. Only then did it occur to me that he might have thought I would cut him out of my life—which I had no intention of doing.

It was several years after my second divorce before I managed to tear myself away from the city I'd been born in and still loved so that I could experience life elsewhere. Because I adored the ocean and disliked hot weather, I would first try San Francisco, I thought. If that did not work out I would try Portland, then, if necessary, Seattle.

Once in San Francisco I was increasingly involved in projects and organizations where I worked alongside lesbians, some gay men, many heterosexual and bisexual women for common goals. In resource files compiled at the time, women offering services were sometimes asked to indicate their sexuality as an optional entry. I believed that women seeking assistance of counselors, dentists, physicians, lawyers, etc. had a right to know, so I wanted to respond, but something in me felt false writing "heterosexual." I finally filled in the blanks with "heterosexual so far."

One day as I walked on a street in the Castro District a youth of twelve or fourteen approached me from the opposite direction. Blond, blue-eyed, neatly dressed, he drew near and suddenly shot a word at me just loud enough for me to hear: "Dyke!" I was certainly startled by what he said, but even more startled by what I said to myself in response: "That's an honor I haven't deserved yet."

Small as the incident was, it revealed to me something about myself and about the respect for lesbians that had been growing in me without my awareness. It helped me understand my need to write "so far" in those resource files.

Comradely affection, sisterly feelings, sometimes even motherly affection (reluctant), and a deep appreciation for the hard work and skills I observed were all part of it. Lesbians were not the only women committed to improving women's live through feminism; but lesbians were always among the best workers when there were specific tasks to be done.

A poem was circulating among members of a collective I belonged to: "How to Make Love to a Woman, if You Are a Woman." I copied it. I read and reread it. I thought, "I could do that." I still thought that becoming a lesbian was essentially about being sexual with women.

COMING OUT

What a diverse set of meanings and implications these two words embody! For someone who believes that being lesbian or gay is inborn, coming out means either releasing to others some knowledge one has always had about oneself or ending "denial" (that is, hiding unconsciously from knowledge of one's sexuality). Others believe that coming out is a choice, but differ among themselves about whether it happens the first time one is aware of being sexually attracted to another of the same sex, perhaps the first time some form of genital sex occurs between them, when a pattern of such relationships is recognized, or when there is a loss of interest in sexual connection with what is usually called the opposite sex. Perhaps each of these is accurate for some of us.

I surely did not think of myself as "coming out" when I decided shortly after my fifty-sixth birthday that I wanted to begin acting on the feelings of attraction to girls, then women, I'd been aware of since adolescence. What I told myself and others in 1975 was that I was "expanding my sexuality." This fit completely with the superficial understandings I'd gleaned at fifteen or sixteen from the psychology shelves in the public library, where I read all the books from Adler to Freud before I stopped. Everybody, I "understood," is born with potential to be bisexual, but the mature choice is to polarize with the opposite sex, and anyone who doesn't is immature. At sixteen I would know the dozen or so girls in my all-female high school who made themselves visible as lesbians. I found them exciting but I was more interested in becoming mature. Besides, I wasn't sexually attracted *only* to girls.

This superficial "understanding" was still with me at fifty-six. I believed that what differentiated lesbians from heterosexuals, provided all were feminists, was that lesbians were sexual exclusively with other women. Since I was not ready (Could I *really* do what that poem described?) to abandon all sexual contact with men, I was not "coming out." Though I knew many lesbians and had been counselor to several, this was only one of my illusions about lesbian lives.

During the next four years I was involved with some women and some men. For some people, perhaps those committed to bisexuality, such a life appears satisfying. As for myself, I felt a growing consternation. It was *not* easy for me to be sexual with a woman. So probably I would never be a lesbian. But I was growing to dislike being sexual with a man. I was not in love with anyone, but did that mean I couldn't be fondly sexual with people I liked? Gradually I became, for the first time in my life, adverse to sex.

Believing as I did that sexual pleasure was good for my and virtually everyone's physical and mental health, I did what any normal person would do and sought a therapist. With the help of some wonderfully perceptive questions and comments on her part I was better able to formulate my situation. No matter how many people can live with double sexual loyalties, I could not. I had finally reached another of the rare times in my life when my philosophy of "both/and" could not be sustained, had to give way to "either/or."

Once I confronted my need to choose, the rest was relatively clear. Sex with a woman was not easy for me? I could trust that with more experience it would become easier, freer, less self-conscious. If "expanding my sexuality" did indeed mean giving up being sexual with men, so be it. Heterosexuality was known territory and was increasingly tedious. I am someone who enjoys challenge, and becoming a lesbian would certainly provide it. I would go forward, not back. That was my first coming out.

COMING OUT TWO

In the next few months I told absolutely everyone I wanted to tell. I still experienced fear at times, and I still had not been sexual with anyone since reaching my decision, but mostly I felt high and happy. People seemed to respond to my excitement more with pleasure than otherwise.

Approximately coinciding with my sixty-first birthday, but without mentioning that connection, I sent out invitations to my "Coming Out Party," a deliberate play on the debutante balls that used to be reported in the society pages of the *New York Times* and other newspapers. I invited everyone I knew who would be willing to celebrate with me, including male friends (a couple of whom had briefly been my lovers). People brought food and drink; some who assumed it was a birthday party also brought gifts. Without undue modesty I can say that I was known as one whose parties were fun to attend. Before the evening was over almost a hundred people had been in my little cottage, some for a short time, some for snacks, some for a long evening of talk and dancing.

Only when it was over and I was alone did I acknowledge that I had cherished hopes for that party, especially that there would be someone who would want to spend the night with me. It seemed a bit unfair that after all the excitement and good wishes and fun I would have to go to bed with a book, but I did. (It was *The Coming Out Stories*, a gift from one of the women I'd been briefly intimate with two years earlier.) Ah, well, it was not the first time in my life that I had gone to bed with a book.

That disappointment did not tarnish my happiness, and it was only the first of many. Truly I wanted to find a woman to love who would love me too. I was convinced that at least part of my sexual unease was that I had not truly loved those I had been with. I joined groups and went everywhere I could think of for social events. At movement events I would initiate conversations or try to dance with any women who looked anywhere near my age.

Gradually I began to think I had wandered into a set of closed circles of women who had known each other for a long time, who were already paired off or were secure within their friendship/social groups. And most of those I met who were around my age had been lesbians either all their lives or for much longer than I. There seemed to be invisible rules of behavior that I could not quite comprehend and therefore repeatedly violated without learning what was wrong—only that something *was* wrong.

I couldn't know, then, that I was being viewed with suspicion, that even my happiness was viewed with suspicion. *They* knew that being lesbian was a tough job. I must have been seen as at best naive, at worst a straight woman playing at being a lesbian.

I was quite aware of having come out into a situation different from what most lesbians my age had encountered. I lived in San Francisco where there were a relatively large number of lesbians. I had lesbian friends with whom I'd worked on women's movement projects and among whom I felt accepted, appreciated, trusted. My family had not abandoned or rejected me. I knew I had to keep coming out as a very *recent* lesbian, however, because assumptions were being made to the contrary based simply on my age. Among age peers, the hardest thing to accept seemed to be that I had come out without having fallen in love with a woman.

COMING OUT THREE

Months earlier, and prior to my decision in the spring, I had applied for and been accepted into a two-trimester training program for experienced therapists; there had been no reason for me to even think of mentioning lesbianism in my application.

Then, fairly soon after my coming out party, I found myself with eight other participants and the instructor, or mentor as he called himself, at a rural retreat center. As we gathered for our first session I scanned the faces and mannerisms of the other four or five women. Were any of them lesbians? It did not occur to me at the time, as it would now, and as it would have then occurred to long-time lesbians my age, to wonder if any of the men were gay. I was relieved that I did not find any of the men particularly attractive, apprehensive that I did feel drawn to one of the women.

I was accustomed to introductory rituals as groups gathered at the first of a projected long series of meetings, but this one was different. We were told we would begin our months of work together by taking half an hour to introduce ourselves. Half an hour! There would be no way to get by with generalities for thirty minutes.

One by one, starting with the mentor, introductions progressed. Selves were disclosed, details of lives, current concerns, physical and emotional anguishes, parts of personal histories. There were three introductions at each session, then we would break for a meal or for quiet time. I was in turmoil throughout, unable to imagine what I would say about myself. I was sitting on top of the biggest and most exciting event in the past several years of my life, and I could not imagine talking about it in this group where each successive self-introduction revealed unquestioning heterosexuality.

At last there was no one else left. I began with statements of appreciation for the openness of each person who had preceded me. Next I said they needed to know there was something important about me I was not ready to disclose yet, but would as soon as I was able. I then talked about everything relevant in my life except my having recently become a lesbian.

During the break that followed we were to remain silent, avoiding conversations with each other, just meditating on all we had heard. Thankful that I would not have to answer questions for a little while, I stripped and jumped into the cold water of the swimming pool (nude swimming was expected at this place). I swam and swam and swam until the heat within me cooled, and then I let myself float belly up. I suddenly thought it rather odd that I was willing to let my naked sixty-one-year-old body be seen by others but not willing to let them see what felt new and wondrous in my soul.

When the group reconvened I was ready to complete my introduction. I told them the process by which I had gotten ready, and then came out to the group.

It was the first of many such comings out, and it taught me a powerful lesson: Coming out in a situation where support cannot be assumed is never, never simple. For the first time I had experienced just a little of what lifelong lesbians have experienced under much more perilous conditions. In this particular situation, having it in the open was a great relief. Two of the women did seem to draw away from me—managed not to sit next to me at meals, for example—but I didn't care. It was very pleasant, on the other hand, to observe but remain out of the heterosexual interplay.

I was present as a lesbian and a feminist and the oldest woman throughout the two academic trimesters. Even the mentor was not much older. Eventually my being a lesbian seemed unimportant to everyone except me. And gradually my feminist challenges to an omnipresent sexism began to gain appreciation.

COMING OUT FOUR

I attended a small national conference on feminist therapy. At a dinner for the sixty of us, a young woman seated several places away from me said to someone in a voice that seemed to ring out, "That's ridiculous! Nobody comes out after sixty." Three years had gone by, and it was much easier for me to say, firmly enough to be heard, "*I* did." I wasn't quite prepared, though, for the attention my response generated.

Questions came at me faster than I could answer any of them. I think I said something like, "I decided it was time to explore the underdeveloped aspects of my sexuality." While this was true, it was partial at best. I might also have said, "I didn't know it at the time but I was hoping to meet and love and be loved by someone who would be my life partner."

Slightly over a year later I thought I had found her. Part of the story of that relationship has been published elsewhere, but it was printed before I discovered that the relationship could not sustain. In a 1987 New Year's letter to friends I wrote that she and I had "parted in love and sorrow." We had not stopped caring for one another, but had found ourselves unable to reconcile important differences. The most important, perhaps, was that I still wanted someone to live with and keep growing old with; she did not want to live with anyone, often said she did not want to grow old.

She was still in her fifties and, like myself at the same age, appeared to prefer dying early to getting old. I think, and hope, that by now she has changed her mind.

COMING OUT FIVE

A few years ago I read a summary of responses by individuals of various ages to the question What is "old"? The summary reported that on the average people under thirty said sixty-three was old; those thirty to thirty-nine said seventy-six; those forty to fifty said seventy; those fifty to fifty-nine said seventy-one; and those over sixty-five said seventy-five was old age. (There was no indication that any one of the respondents identified his or her own age as old.)

Another sign of ageism appeared in an issue of *Modern Maturity* in 1986 or 1987 under a modest heading, "Let's Change the Word 'Elderly.' " The writer suggested that though many people are happy with "elderly" or "senior citizen," others are not. For those who disliked those two designations, the writer suggested substituting the word "emeritan." The one word not worthy of consideration was, of course, *old*.

In 1987 I told my beloved eighty-two-year-old aunt that I would be participating in the first West Coast Conference and Celebration of Old Lesbians. My aunt responded that she herself did not "feel the least bit old." "Old is not a feeling," I answered. "It is a fact of life and I refuse to be ashamed of being old."

As I passed through the doors to the room where the 1987 Old Lesbian Conference was just starting on a Friday night, about two hundred lesbians were seated in small groups around tables, laughing and talking, probably meeting old friends and making new ones. To me, as I stood in the doorway, there appeared to be an ocean of gray and white hair, dotted with other colors. I thought of the largely hidden histories this room now contained; my eyes flooded, and emotion took my breath away.

The next morning I was able to speak my gratitude to those in the audience who had lived and struggled and built the movements that made it possible for women like me to enter later in life and with far less struggle. Participation in organizing this conference helped me find the community of age peers I had been seeking. It is not the only "community" in which I participate, but it is one indispensable to my well-being.

A number of us who were Northern California lesbians wanted to create a successor event in our area. We presented a proposal to the closure meeting of the 1987 Planning Committee, and it was accepted. The two hundred dollars or so left in the treasury was turned over to us as seed money, along with the list of registrants. Again it required two years of collective work and meetings, but in 1989 the second West Coast Conference of Old Lesbians took place.

By then we had heard that a National Lesbian Conference would be held, probably in Atlanta, in a year or two. Based on our individual experiences we believed we would not feel welcome there unless something was done to prevent the invisibility of old lesbians.

About fifty of the participants at the 1989 conference signed on for what was to be called an Old Lesbian Organizing Committee, specifically to assure a strong and vocal old lesbian presence at the Atlanta meeting.

Prior to the first conference I feared I would again have to defend my situation as a lesbian by choice, and a choice made relatively late in life. The opposite happened. In fact, the workshops and consciousness-raising sessions at *both* conferences highlighted how different our lives had been up to that point. Far from preventing unity among us, those differences seemed to increase our ability to accept, respect and value each other and ourselves.

The spirit carried numbers of us from around the country to Atlanta in 1991. It has survived in an ongoing organization now known as Old Lesbians Organized for Change, OLOC for short. OLOC now has regional groups around the country.

This article cannot begin to encompass the breadth and depth of what I have gained since choosing, in 1980, to "go forward, not back" by making a commitment to a lesbian life. I have learned and continue to learn what it means to be committed to women. I have been accepted by a sufficient number of lesbians; I don't worry any more about acceptance by those who have different definitions.

I don't believe I was "always a lesbian" waiting to discover myself as such, but maybe I was. It doesn't seem to matter these days. I've read and reflected considerably on issues of human sexuality, and have reached the belief that sexuality is a continuum. I visualize a long, long line of women (all women because I'm not at all sure my image reflects male sexuality). At one end are gathered the women who seem to be biochemically/hormonally unable to experience sexual attraction or gratification with women. At the other end are women who seem to be biochemically or hormonally unable to experience sexual attraction or gratification *except* with women.

Between the ends and the center are women for whom life experience and social pressure, starting in childhood, determine sexuality. All the rest of us choose, whether freely or because of an imposed heterosexual norm, whether gladly or with pain and doubt, what our sexuality will be. Our choices may be conscious or unconscious. Also in this heavily populated middle are women, the true bisexuals perhaps, who have chosen both—as well as those who opt for a nonsexual life.

My place is in this middle. I made one choice in my youth, then found I could make another choice later in life.

As I write this essay I am newly in love and in a relationship with an exciting and passionate woman who proudly claims the word "old." We live and work four hours driving distance apart. Both of us must continue to work several years more if we hope to maintain ourselves in even modest comfort.

It is too soon to know how permanent this relationship will be, but not too soon to know that each of us offers the other some shared and some contentious values. Even by the time this book is out, it may have ended. The future is unknown; and though the present is often challenging, sometimes even difficult, it is also a time of great joy.

CHAPTER 2

How I Found My Way Home:
Confessions of an Older Gay Man

BY

R. BERGER

About the Author: Raymond M. Berger studied clinical psychology at the State University of New York at Stony Brook, where he graduated with a B.S., summa cum laude, in 1972. While at Stony Brook he was involved in various research projects on concept formation in children and adults. He also led community preparation training sessions for chronically mentally ill patients at Central Islip State Hospital.

Berger earned his master's degree in social work and his doctorate in social welfare at the University of Wisconsin, Madison, where he also served as a lecturer. During his master's program he specialized in school social work and helped organize and staff a multipurpose volunteer center for gay men. As a doctoral student, and later as an adjunct faculty member, he began to study older persons. His dissertation research, funded by a grant he submitted to the Administration on Aging, presented the first application of assertion training to nursing-home residents. He continued to work with nursing-home residents under a grant he authored that was funded by the National Institutes of Mental Health. He later became a nursing-home consultant.

From 1977 to 1979 Berger served as assistant professor of social work at Florida International University in Miami. There he organized an innovative support group for older gay men for which he was given the Human Rights Award of the Dade County Coalition for Human Rights in 1979. He also began the research that led to his ground-breaking book, *Gay and Gray: The Older Homosexual Man* (University of Illinois Press, 1982; reprinted by Alyson Publications, 1984). *Gay and Gray* was the first academic study to present a realistic picture of older gay men's life situations, and in 1982 it received the prestigious Evelyn Hooker Award of the Gay Academic Union.

As an associate professor of social work at the University of Illinois at Urbana-Champaign from 1980 to 1985, Berger coauthored two popular research textbooks for social work and human service students. He also worked as an individual and family therapist at the Champaign County Mental Health Center while continuing his research and writing on the elderly and on gay men and lesbians. In 1985 he was listed in *International Authors and Writers Who's Who* (tenth edition).

From 1986 to 1991 he was a full professor of social work at California State University, Long Beach, where he continued his research and writing about older persons and about gays and lesbians. While there he originated a unique writing-development program for minority and women faculty: The Getting Published Program assisted faculty in achieving publication of their scholarly works. He also conducted national research on the writing skills and problems of academic faculty. In recognition of his teaching, research, and publications, he received the University's Meritorious Performance and Professional Promise Award as well as the Distinguished Faculty Scholarly and Creative Achievement Award.

Berger currently lives in a small rural community that's dedicated to self-reliance and ecological harmony.

λ

So you are a gay man of a "certain age," as the French say. Me too. (I'm in my forties.) This business of aging has been a bit of an embarrassment for me. You see, as a young professor I made a career of studying older gay men. I promoted the idea that gay aging does not have to be bleak and dreary, and I often gave advice about ways in which gay men could cope with growing older. I always said it could be done with dignity. Now I've got to prove it.

I've learned that each person marches to a different tune. All I can do is describe the music I've heard along my own path. So in this chapter I'll tell you what I have experienced as I've gotten older.

OLD: WHO, ME?

When do we stop being a "young person"? When I was in my twenties I remember an elderly gay gentleman telling me, "I know I may be old and wrinkled on the outside, but on the inside I'm still twenty." Now I think I understand what he meant.

Perhaps I was naive, but as a teenager I imagined being old in a very different way. From my youthful perspective I believed that when I became older I would be more self-confident, make decisions easily, and feel settled in my career and relationships. I now know that life never settles down; that I still feel weak in difficult moments; that important decisions are rarely easy.

While some of my perspectives have changed, I'm essentially the same person I always was. I've had a few hardships along the way (gotten ill, lost loved ones to AIDS, ended unhappy relationships), but maybe I survived *because* I continued to be the same person. The single constant denominator has been my identity, my sense of self. This is who I am, nothing has ever changed that, and nothing will—so perhaps I'll get through this life after all.

Still, it was a shock to realize that my youth was behind me. Recently I read a report that described me as a "well-groomed middle-aged man." I cringed. "Is it really time," I thought, "to think of myself as middle-aged?" It still seems that label should only be applied to parents, aunts and uncles, and schoolteachers.

I know I'm not alone in my reaction. The gerontological literature on "age-status labeling" shows that even those of us who are in our seventies or eighties dislike calling ourselves "old." Gay men realize they are no longer "young" by the time they reach forty, but no matter how much older they get, they are unlikely to call themselves "old."

I suspect that the age we identify as "old" creeps forward as the definer gets older. I was reminded of that a few years ago on a visit to my parents, who live in a retirement community whose residents have become quite elderly. I overheard this conversation:

"Did you hear that Larry died?"

"Oh no. How old was he?"

"Eighty-nine."

"My, he was so young!"

MY BODY, MYSELF

Long before I dreamed of calling myself middle-aged I remember being unhappy with physical changes in my body. I spent my twenties being the perennial graduate student; I kept my nose in the books, got little physical exercise.

The first thing I noticed was those much-maligned "love handles." My slim waist became a little less slim. Then the physical fitness craze of the 1980s happened and I tried running, swimming—even a short adventure with weights. But it was too late. The fat cells refused to budge. There were other changes too: Lines sprouted around my eyes and on my forehead, and the skin under my jaws became looser.

Years later I found myself gasping, "Oh no!" as my morning mirror revealed an area of thinning hair on top of my head. I always prized my full head of hair. So this seemed the ultimate indignity. I worried about it getting worse.

I had to come to terms with these changes.

What was I scared of? I worried that if I lost my good looks I would no longer be attractive to other gay men. But I knew that wasn't true.

I knew that certain physical qualities can be very attractive even if most people do not consider them so. For example my friend Rosita is *only* attracted to balding men with beer bellies—perhaps because these features remind her of her husband, whom she adores. But there are attractive qualities that go beyond the physical.

How many times had I been attracted to other people because of personal qualities—warmth, honesty, or competence—rather than physical appearance? And if these qualities made others more desirable to me, wasn't that also true of the way others saw me?

I had a particularly enlightening conversation with my mirror one day. I thought, I am angry that my good looks are going away. Boy, when I was young, I was really cute. I wish I had realized it then; I would have enjoyed my appearance. Instead, I always felt like an ugly duckling.

Then I had a flash. I was still looking into my mirror. But this time I was a very old man, and I thought, Boy, I was sure cute when I was middle-aged. I wish I had realized it back then; I would have enjoyed my appearance.

To me, one of the nicest things about growing older is that I am finally beginning to like myself. I know I have a choice: I can enjoy who I am *at this very moment* and make my life peaceful and fulfilled. Or I can fret about the things that don't seem "right" and make my life frustrating and unhappy. I still marvel at this choice, which I never before knew I had.

"WILL YOU TALK TO ME?"

Most of the older gay men in my research studies believed that younger gay men wanted nothing to do with them. I'm not sure why I knew better even before I did my research. Perhaps it was because there were a few older men who were very attractive to me. Or perhaps it was because I was drawn to older people and loved to hear their stories about the past. Or maybe it was because I knew there were many young gay men who longed for a relationship with an older man, one who would replace the loving father they never had.

Despite this, I am sure every older gay man has, at some time, been rejected by a young gay man. The first time it happened to me, I was surprised. At a small party I had approached an attractive young man—perhaps in his early twenties—and we held a pleasant conversation. But the young man must have felt my interest was more serious than it really was; he blurted out, "All the men interested in me are too old. I want to relate to people my own age." I assumed I fell in the "too old" category.

I was annoyed. At the same time I appreciated his honesty. How sad, I thought, that he will not get to know a great many people who might offer him friendship, support, and more. For a time I felt wounded. After all, wasn't I the one who had been rejected?

But my never-to-be friend had not rejected me, because he never got to know me. The loss was his. And it was his loss to repeat over and over again, until he learned that people are important for who they really are, rather than for the number of birthdays they have celebrated.

HAVING A LOVER

Last year I joined a support group for gay men in their forties and fifties. When we discussed what each of us wanted in our lives, I was surprised to learn that everyone else in the group wanted a lover. I was the only one who was uncertain.

The year before, I had decided *not* to have a lover. I was just ending a stormy relationship with Gary, a very decent and devoted man who had given me lots of support when I became ill with chronic fatigue syndrome. But I was determined to move far away to the country, to heal myself, since I had become sensitive to air pollution in the city where we lived.

Because we cared so deeply for each other, the breakup was difficult. I just did not have the heart to think about starting a relationship with someone new. Besides, as a person with a chronic illness—and as the only gay person living in a small rural community—prospects did not seem bright for meeting the right person. Most importantly, I had seen the terrible stress my illness had created for Gary:

enduring my inability to share normal activities like nights out on the town, my depression during flare-ups, my periods of withdrawal. It seemed easier to be on my own.

Now I'm beginning to reevaluate. As an older and more mature man, in many ways I am better prepared than I was in my younger years to nurture a good relationship. First of all, I know that being with a lover is no substitute for having a purposeful and rewarding life; having a lover won't make an unfulfilled life worthwhile. So I never wait around for Mr. Right. Instead I try to surround myself with good friends, to be productive doing the things I love to do, and to have dreams for my future.

In the past I attracted men into my life who were often unkind or who didn't share my values. I would have crushes and be willing to mold my interests to theirs or try to make myself into the kind of person they wanted.

As an older man, I'm different. I no longer let just anyone into my life. A good-looking man is always a treat, but looks alone won't cut it. Is he interested in and informed about the things that interest me? Is he concerned about the world around him? Is he genuine, honest with others and with himself? Does he feel good enough about himself that he avoids the need to judge others? Is he compassionate? Does my heart tell me this is a person I want to be close to? These are the things I look for in a friend *or* a lover. When I don't find people with these qualities, I choose to be alone.

When I was younger I could scan a row of guys at a bar and tell you which ones I liked and which I didn't like. Now my tastes are more fluid. I can still appreciate an attractive young man, but I might not choose to spend time with him. Many times I have met men who did not seem at all attractive to me. But after I got to know them, learned to appreciate their warmth or other qualities, they became very attractive to me.

It's all in my attitude. I believe it is possible for all of us, at any age, to learn to see beneath the surface into the more real and rewarding parts of the people we meet. I think of that now as looking into others' souls.

As an older gay man I look back and realize that for much of my adult life I did have a lover. That is I had several lovers, and I usually shared a home and most of my free time with that lover. But if I were with a lover today I would ask myself, Is this really the person I want to be with? Can I accept the ways in which he does not measure up to my ideal of what a lover should be? Are there things about my lover that will bring us closer as we grow old together?

After all, as I get older I realize that life is short and not to be wasted. If an intimate relationship does not bring fulfillment into my life, I need to either work to make it better or change the nature of that relationship so it does not drain my energy and compassion.

DOES MY STORY HAVE A HAPPY ENDING?

I think so. And it also shows that there are creative solutions to the dilemma of being on one's own.

For years I have been attracted to the idea of being part of a family. I even spent a couple of months living in an "intentional community" in the mountains where we worked, ate, and played together. But community living was too intense for me, and the rural isolation made it difficult for me to pursue my career. So I moved to my own little house out in the country. I was lucky enough to find a gay men's support group where I touched souls with half a dozen others living in nearby rural areas.

Then a wonderful thing happened. I became friends with Dave, one of the members of the support group. Dave is a divorced man of about my age who has a teenage daughter. I began to spend time with Dave and Sara, becoming a regular guest in their home. I got to know Dave's mom and dad, and we hit it off. I knew Dave longed for adult companionship, but I was still surprised when one day he invited me to move into his large house. Since I also wanted companionship, and since Dave and Sara seemed just like the family I had always wanted, I agreed.

Dave warned me that being part of a family is stressful at times. He was right. I have had to learn how to play the difficult role of stepparent to a teenager whose behavior I don't always understand. Both Dave and I have moods, and there are times when we disagree about everything from proper diet to household chores. The bright side is that I have learned how to be more trusting, how to have a productive conflict with someone I care about and end up loving him even more. (I'm not sure I'll ever get the stepparent role down right; I'm working on that one!)

Dave and I are two gay men who share almost every part of our lives together, but we are not lovers. I suppose there are those who say that what we have is wrong or artificial.

But we feel we have arrived at a happy destination.

WHEN I GROW UP I WANT TO BE ...

I guess most people have a fantasy about the kind of job or career they would like. Often that fantasy is very different from the fact.

I have been lucky. Until recently I spent most of my adult life doing work I loved: being a university professor. When I started out in my late twenties I was determined to learn and teach about gay men and women, and that is just what I did. But I also found that the life of a university professor can be very stressful and competitive, and those aspects of my work often made me unhappy. So, like many young people starting out in new careers, I fantasized that I could always try another career—something "completely different"—even if that meant going to school again, or starting from the bottom.

For me, growing older has meant facing a scary truth: It is becoming less and less likely that I will ever launch into a new career.

I must make the best of what I've got. (That seems to be a lesson that goes far beyond my choice of work.)

In some ways these career issues are no different from those experienced by all older men, gay or straight. But an older gay man may face a situation that is a bit different from the norm. Recently I asked a gay friend, a banker in his late forties, if he felt his lack of a college degree had kept him from advancing in his career. He held out his hand, pointing to a finger without a wedding band, and commented, "Not as much as being unmarried." Particularly in rural and conservative areas, an older gay professional may feel that prejudice and misunderstanding about his homosexuality have hindered his career. It is a frustrating situation. It is also one that is difficult to solve, because a career change becomes more difficult as one gets older.

But an older gay man may also have career advantages over his heterosexual counterpart. A job or career change may be easier for the gay man without family or children. Free of family obligations, a gay man is better able to relocate, freer to choose to return to school or temporarily give up income, in order to achieve a more satisfying career.

I experienced a dramatic "career change" at the age of forty-one. I became disabled. I am no longer able to hold down a job—at least not now. But I am still able to think, to argue my beliefs, and to continue writing well enough to create essays like this one that I hope are worth reading. It hasn't been easy. What I used to do in a couple of hours may now take a couple of months. But that has taught me patience. It has allowed me to savor the experiences more slowly, and to appreciate that every task holds joy and learning if only I give it the respect it deserves. In other words, I no longer endure "busy work." Everything I do is important because I am able to do it, and I care about doing it well.

That brings me to the most important thing I have learned about work: The quality of my experience is not determined by *what* I do, but rather by how I do it.

I am glad now that in my earlier life I chose to do the work I loved rather than the work that was supposed to enhance my career. As a graduate student, and again as a young professor, I was warned by concerned friends not to specialize in studying gay people, because that would ruin my career. Later I chose to develop a program to help minority and women faculty members write scholarly articles. The nay-sayers appeared once again. They said my work was trivial and unimportant. But I persevered because I loved doing it, and I saw that it helped many aspiring young professors. If I had listened to my well-meaning colleagues I would never have enjoyed my career as much as I did. I would not have the wonderful memories that have helped me get through the difficulty of my forced retirement. And I might still not know how to do the work I love, not to love the work I do.

HOW I FOUND MY WAY HOME

Sometimes I imagine myself in the moments before my birth. God allows me the privilege of previewing the life that lies ahead, although I know I will forget all of this when I am born, that I'll have to learn my lessons all over. But just now I am horrified at my prospects. I'll be born to two middle-aged parents, survivors of Nazi concentration camps, who are traumatized from losing their families in the war. They will struggle to make it in a strange country where they don't know the language or the customs. At the age of six I will lose my only sibling and begin to have nightmares of guilt, of death, of being hunted by enemies. As an adolescent I will struggle with the confusion and terror of feelings I can't understand. I will choose to live as a gay person, and that will bring love, but also a fight for survival. Later I will experience the frustration of one failed relationship after another. The stress will mount until I am diagnosed with a debilitating and apparently incurable illness. I will be old before my time. I will collapse. I will start over.

I protest to God. "No, this incarnation is too difficult. I'm sure I don't need to learn that many lessons." But this is idle talk. My life begins.

I am certain I would not have chosen these experiences. Still, something remarkable has happened. I was raised in a home with few religious or spiritual values by parents who believed that God had either abandoned them or didn't exist. I did not know I was living in a spiritual void until I grew older and felt something missing: a purpose, a center, meaning. Being gay, growing older, falling ill; these things led me, slowly, painfully, persistently, to my center. To my beliefs.

This is what I believe. My essence, my true identity, is not my body. It is my soul. And that soul is eternal. My soul experiences many lifetimes, and those lifetimes provide lessons to enhance the development of my soul. Therefore there is a purpose for every event and feeling I experience. The ultimate destination of my soul is unity with God. God is not an individual, but the unity of all things that are.

Granted, these ideas are abstract. But they help put my life in context. There is a reason why we humans are separated into gay and straight, young and old, black and white, male and female. These sometimes painful differences exist to teach us our lessons, to help us explore the wonder of our many aspects—and eventually to learn that we are all one.

To me, the most important part of my spiritual journey has been learning that I belong. I never thought I belonged. I started out as a refugee, a scrawny kid who couldn't speak English properly, someone who didn't fit into his family or at school. I always felt out of place. Now I know that whatever I am, whatever I am doing, I belong. Not only do I belong, *I am an essential part* of creation. All my experiences, the joy *and* the pain, have a purpose.

So what am I to make of my aging? It is just an experience. An essential experience that will mature not just my body, but my soul too, freeing it eventually to unite with God.

On a practical level, I believe I must never use age as an excuse to avoid doing what I am meant to do. And how often we do just that! For example, several years ago I spent a summer pursuing my dream of living in an intentional community (a group of about forty people who lived in the country and shared all resources, income and labor). Even after I returned to the city I was so filled with joy at my experience that for the first few days I spoke to almost everyone I met about what I had experienced.

I especially remember two of my encounters. One was a meeting with my insurance agent, a businesswoman in her fifties. After hearing my story, she surprised me by pulling out an obviously treasured medicine bag filled with healing crystals. She confided to me that she too harbored a lifelong dream of living in a spiritual community in the mountains. But that was impossible, she said. "For an older person like me, there are too many ties to job and family to leave the city. Only a younger person, someone with less to lose, could leave his life and join a community."

Later that day I talked to my auto mechanic, a man in his early twenties, recently married, with a new child. To my surprise his eyes lit up when I described my experiences that summer. My mechanic told me how he dreamed of leaving the dangerous and stressful city for a better life in the country. "But for a young person like me, who isn't yet established, someone with a family and not a lot of money, that's impossible. Only an older person, someone more settled, could do that."

From this I learned that my dreams are only there when I catch them.

After a time I left the city.

It wasn't easy. I left behind my lover, who was just becoming ill with AIDS. My joy at pursuing my dream, at having the opportunity to heal from my own illness, was tempered by the grief of losing Gary.

One day I called Gary at home and heard his mother's voice instead of his. I braced myself to hear the bad news. Gary was in the hospital again; it looked very bad. I knew he didn't have much time left, and I knew I could not be there with him. The grief began to hit me in waves. I was all alone in my little house in the forest and I did not know how to grieve. Instinctively I bolted out the door and ran into the woods. I walked quickly, not paying attention to my direction or to the late hour.

I walked until I was exhausted before I noticed it was getting dark. Suddenly I panicked. I had no idea where I was or in what direction home was. I knew I was probably miles from any house or road. It began to look like I would have to spend the night in the woods. My fear increased. Filled with anxiety and grief I gave up, collapsing onto a rocky ledge.

Just as I hit the ground, I saw a streak of fur through the trees, and in an instant my friend Azalon was licking at my grateful hands. Azalon was a German shepherd that belonged to neighbors and with whom I had spent many happy hours.

As Azalon patiently led me home, I realized I was going to survive this loss. I learned that no matter how great my pain, or how alone and frightened I feel, I have only to remember.

Sooner or later we all find our way home.

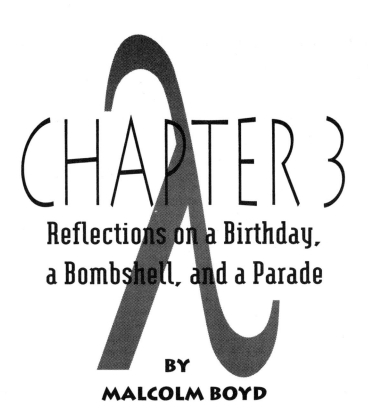

CHAPTER 3

Reflections on a Birthday, a Bombshell, and a Parade

BY

MALCOLM BOYD

About the Author: In the 1940s a youthful Malcolm Boyd became film star Mary Pickford's partner in a production company and was elected president of the Television Producers Association of Hollywood. In the 1950s he entered a seminary and was ordained an Episcopal priest. The *New York Times Magazine* later described him as "a latter-day Luther or a more worldly Wesley, trying to move organized religion out of 'ghettoized' churches into the streets—where people are." In the 1960s his best-selling book, *Are You Running with Me, Jesus?* (Beacon, 1990), appeared and he became a leader in the civil rights and peace movements.

Life included him in its cover story on "The Take-Over Generation." *Mademoiselle* named him a "Disturber of the Peace" with James Baldwin, Norman Mailer, and Federico Fellini. He spoke on the nation's campuses, gave public readings of his work, appeared for a month at San Francisco's legendary hungry i, and became a fellow at Yale. In the 1970s he was a principal speaker at the Bicentennial of American Law at New York University School of Law. He was honored by an invitation to reside at Mishkenot Sha'ananim, the center for artists and writers in Jerusalem. Boston University established the Malcolm Boyd Collection.

A newsmagazine described him (September 27, 1976) as "blunt, restless, eloquent and above all, open"; yet it also noted that "he has kept one aspect of his life deeply private: his homosexuality." Boyd had just announced that he is gay.

In the 1980s he became writer-priest-in-residence at St. Augustine-by-the-Sea Episcopal Church in Santa Monica, California, and served three terms as president of PEN Center U.S.A. West. The author of twenty-two books, he also served on the national council of the Fellowship of Reconciliation, the nation's oldest peace organization, and visited the Soviet Union as a member of a peace delegation in May 1987. He was named a member of the Los Angeles City/County AIDS Task Force.

In the 1990s Boyd became chaplain of the commission on AIDS Ministry of the Episcopal Diocese of Los Angeles. *Are Your Running with Me, Jesus?* appeared in a twenty-fifth anniversary edition, a new book, *Edges, Boundaries, and Connections* (Broken Moon Press, 1992) was published, a revised edition of Boyd's classic work *Take Off the Masks* (Harper Collins, 1993) was planned, and he started work on another new book, *Rich with Years* (Harper Collins, 1993). He also celebrated the thirty-fifth anniversary of his ordination as an Episcopal priest. Boyd lives in Los Angeles with his life partner, Mark Thompson, longtime senior editor of *The Advocate* and author of *Gay Spirit: Myth and Meaning* (St. Martin's Press, 1987), an anthology to which Boyd contributed.

J une 8. These are a few lines I placed on paper and sent to a few friends about today's sixty-ninth birthday:

This June 8th I'm sixty-nine.
So next June 8th I'm—oops!—seventy.
How did that happen?
Isn't anyone here in charge?
Let's form a committee and look into this situation.
What if I want to reverse the trend?
Next June 8th, what if I want to be sixty-eight?
Fifty-eight? Forty-eight? Thirty-eight? Twenty-eight? No, thanks, on eighteen or eight.
Give me a breather before it's eighty, okay?
Life resembles a roller coaster. I mean, it's moving.
Fast.
Faster.
Fastest.
Some yuppie thinks he or she understands the fast lane.
Ha!
I think I'll retreat to a quiet monastery.
Fountains of water splashing gently in the courtyard.
A voice is never raised.
Everything is quietly and perfectly in order.
There are no problems.
Time stops.
On second thought, give me the fast lane.
Sixty-nine is okay.
Seventy will certainly be interesting.
Are you running with me, Jesus?

For nearly forty years I have been an Episcopal priest. For the past decade I have labored in the vineyard of St.

Augustine-by-the-Sea in Santa Monica, California, and will officially retire when I am seventy and a half. Of course, since junior high school I have been a writer and will continue as such.

My birthday conjures up images of mortality. Why not? The major part of my life lies behind me. Many close friends have already departed. And, I encounter mortality when I regard my mother, who is going on ninety-five. She is also remarkable, a role model of intelligent and sensitive aging. Beatrice manages to stay bright, resilient, self-sufficient, caring, and hopeful. A salvific sense of humor matches her tough survival skills. Beatrice lives alone with two fish, a lemon tree, an orange tree, and helpful neighbors nearby.

The other key figure in my life is Mark, my lover and life partner. For fifteen years he has been an editor of *The Advocate*, the national gay and lesbian newsmagazine, and is the author of two celebrated books, *Gay Spirit: Myth and Meaning* and *Leatherfolk*. We find that being two writers under one roof works splendidly for us.

At forty Mark is a man deeply committed to the well-being of earth and the sacredness of friendship. He is a quintessential Leo: easygoing, steady, a veritable rock of Gibraltar. Surprisingly I encounter the reality of mortality when I regard Mark, too, because he is HIV positive and has the AIDS virus.

It was a bombshell the day we found out. I jotted down these lines, addressed to Mark, to describe my initial reaction.

It had been a busy afternoon and I got caught up in all kinds of details and telephone calls. In fact, I was on the phone when I heard you walk in the front door.

There you stood looking at me. I glanced up and smiled. But when I saw your eyes, I knew something was terribly wrong. I ended the call in a few seconds.

"I've just tested positive for HIV," you said.

The big ship seemed to shudder after hitting an iceberg. Everything was changed in a moment. I felt chilled, wary. Were years dropping away like cards in a deck? My mind raced: Will you die of AIDS? Will you suffer? Have KS? Pneumocystis? My thoughts focused abstractly on healing, T-cells, vitamins, alternative treatments, and cutting down stress.

The house stayed so still. In a short while we faced one another across a table. You had always wanted to grow old, you said. Become one of those wonderful old men who are wise and beautiful and caring, and whom people love.

But now, you said, you might not have the chance. What if there were only three years. Four years.

As I went over to hold you my reality changed, dreams shifted. My sense of timing seemed off, out of sync, like the anarchic melody in Ravel's **La Valse.** *The waltz had changed.*

Mark believes his entire life is a preparation for the single act of dying, which is inseparable from life; it's the springboard for moving into the next step of his existence.

His spiritual base is Buddhism. he has also been deeply influenced by Jungian therapy. Always strongly supportive,

Mark loves attending church with me two or three times a year—to hear me preach on a special occasion and, always, for the luminous beauty of the candlelit Christmas Eve midnight mass. Meanwhile, often I try out my sermons on him at home as we're seated quietly before the hearth, and I faithfully read and offer constructive criticism about his writings on leatherfolk and radical faeries.

I love him dearly and cannot imagine my life without him. Yet it is entirely possible he will be gone unless a cure is found for AIDS. Or, given my seniority, Mark may outlive me.

AIDS has demythologized death a great deal for me. I've come to perceive death as a process, a part of living. I find it is not so much an individual matter; indeed, it's a singular part of our human commonality. People are dying in every part of the world all the time. Each one of us is always in the process of living and dying, dying and living.

So, I realize my own death (when it comes) will not stop any clocks. Hopefully it won't be an occasion for mourning, but a moment of quiet celebration by those who care.

AIDS has radically changed my view of life. We have the present moment. *Live it.* Play it as an instrument. Bake it as a cake. Water it as a plant. Adore it, honor it, fulfill it. Let yesterday go; don't remain a prisoner forever in an outworn structure. Let tomorrow come if it will; how, when and where.

Today, however, has a sacred quality. Most of my life I avoided the sacredness, wonder, and pleasure of the moment. I was restless and in a hurry to get beyond the present to the next place, the enticing future. This is true no longer. Finally I comprehend the sense of a famous ad for a steamship line: Getting there is half the fun. Half the meaning. So, it's the journey that occupies me now. The journey that offers those tantalizing forks in the road. The journey that is in the present.

None of us is an island. Our lives are interconnected. Certainly Mark's and mine are. We're in life together. That we share the present moment with one another is God's gift. The meaning of this concerning AIDS is striking and unmistakable. Our response, Mark's and mine, to AIDS must be to live in the present, help one another, and participate in meeting the needs of our wider community.

The Talmud says: "One who destroys a single life, it is as if one destroys the entire world. One who saves a single life, it is as if one saves the entire world." Jesus identifies the stranger, the prisoner, the outcast, the hungry, the sick *as himself*. From across the centuries the prophet Amos tells us to "establish justice." Where is justice in terms of AIDS? It can only be found in stopping the deaths. Saving the lives of men, women, and children. Stemming horrible human suffering. Caring compassionately for those who suffer, and meeting their needs. Finding a cure.

In order to keep going I have to continually revitalize my faith and spiritual imagination, stir up my hope and love, somehow discover resources of the spirit to wind up my energy anew.

June 29: Yesterday I rode on the back of a shiny red convertible in the twenty-second annual festive parade that marks Los Angeles's Gay and Lesbian Pride Celebration. A quarter of a million people lined the parade route. Waving at thousands and thousands of them I noticed a large number of older lesbians and gay men. I identified particularly with them because we belong to the same age group.

It got me thinking: As older gay people, what are our major concerns? I don't think they include making a million dollars, earning world-class fame, building the next skyscraper, or writing a book that outsells the Bible. In no particular order I believe they include health, financial security, friendships, networking, and meaning.

We older gays are generally strong people for the simple reason that we've survived long decades of homophobia and its side effects. Sure, some of us have fallen by the wayside. One is a guy I know whom I'll call Bill. He stumbled into alcoholism. I found him at home one afternoon. He sat naked at a kitchen table. With him was a six-pack of beer and a gallon jug of warm white wine. He blurted out, "I don't like you to find me this way." Yet "this way" held a lot of truth about him. A gifted and sensitive man, he had simply given up, surrendering to his feelings of inadequacy and fear. His self-esteem was so low it wouldn't have covered his shoes if he'd been wearing any.

Bill is like a number of older gays who never experienced the positive aspects of the gay and lesbian community because they remained rigidly closeted, self-hating, isolated, and lonely. There is nothing worse than to suffer beneath the weight of the twin stereotypes of being "old" and "homosexual." Both have long ago been consigned to the trash heap by many of us, yet others remain imprisoned. Terrible feelings caused by homophobia are internalized, and then projected onto other gays. Bitter thoughts are harbored, and they fester spiritually. A malaise of lovelessness gives way to reclusiveness.

It doesn't help when the gay community becomes obsessed by youth culture and engages in age-bashing. Older gays and lesbians need to feel accepted, enabled to feel the security of companionship that crosses barriers of age and gender. It is beneficial when older gays and lesbians are offered, and accept, mentoring roles *vis-à-vis* younger counterparts. It is helpful to experience the liberation of lesbian and gay pride. It is important to perceive the dignity, wisdom and peace of aging as well as its obvious problems.

I know many, many older lesbians and gay men who handle their lives beautifully. They live in healthy, happy relationships; mentor younger people; participate in community activities; sometimes play leadership roles; continue to be creative about living. How well do older gay folk take care of the major concerns I listed earlier?

Health comes first. Speaking for myself, I take very good care of my body. I see others doing the same thing, especially those accustomed to working out at a gym. I walk regularly at a quick, steady pace, up and down sharp inclines that make my heart beat faster. I swim passionately, with real verve and fervor. I love getting in the water, more so if it's the ocean. I am under the care of an excellent doctor and an excellent dentist, both of whom I visit faithfully.

In money matters many of us were Depression kids. I remember when my family lost everything in 1929 and the early 1930s. I became accustomed to frugality and occasional hunger. Those of us who shared this experience of limitation and loss naturally tend to be prudent and wise about money. We know it does not grow on trees. Also, we remember when a postage stamp cost three cents, there were hamburgers for a dime, and a kid got into a movie for a quarter. Believe me, this provides a conservative perspective on today's spiraling costs and easy-come, easy-go money.

Friendships are, I think, the most precious gifts in the world. Lesbians and gays know their value in a world that was often unfriendly. Many years ago an older gay couple, two men living in a longtime relationship, offered me friendship when I was beginning to come to terms with being gay. I desperately needed their understanding support, experience and presence in my life. They provided it unstintingly. I am forever grateful to them. Now I have the opportunity to return their gift by offering my friendship to younger lesbians and gay men who need the same things they gave me. A corollary of friendship is networking. It's about the outreach and involvement of our lives. For example, there is community participation. Volunteerism. Dialogue with other people about matters of common concern. Being a part of decision making. Networking is the exact opposite of isolation and loneliness.

Meaning? It's as necessary to me as oxygen. Food, drink, sex, and money are not enough for me. I've got to come face-to-face with a new challenge. I need a fresh human need to meet. I yearn for an unexpected mountain to climb. I absolutely require a compelling reason to greet a new day with cheer and energy.

I find that many older lesbians and gay men I know feel the same way I do. Riding yesterday in the bright red convertible in the exciting Gay and Lesbian Pride Celebration parade, waving enthusiastically to thousands of people who lined the route, I felt happy about being gay *and* older. I am grateful for my life up to this moment: Being gay is a part of who I am in God's creation, and so a blessing. Being older is a new challenge, and a blessing.

July 9. On July Fourth Mark and I barbecued and invited a friend to join us. He is a member of our extended family. An older gay man, he lives alone since his life partner's death due to AIDS.

I was reminded once again of the significance of the extended family for lesbians and gay men. We know "family values" very well. We preserve them. Too, we understand fully the words in the traditional marriage ceremony, "in sickness and in health." For older gays the extended family renders possible a sense of community and its corollary of shared experiences. Being secretive about one's gayness and remaining in the closet mitigates against the possibility of joining an extended family, celebrating life with happiness and fulfillment.

During my life I've known dozens of closeted lesbians and gay men. The dank, claustrophobic closet often separated them from relaxed, open sharing with potential companions and friends.

I know a distinguished bishop, a closeted gay man, who lives a classic split life. First there is the prestigious, busy public life; his appointment book is organized a full year in advance. Always he seems surrounded by a veritable army of active people. Second, however, there is the utter solitariness of his private life. He feels he cannot share "the secret" of his sexual orientation with friends and associates. Existing atop an ecclesiastical pedestal, he does not know how to accept his own humanity or share human intimacy. Yet I'm convinced an unmistakable irony contributes to his evident sharp feelings of guilt: While he is telling others how to live, he has not found a way to translate such wisdom to the barren pages of his own interior life.

Let me introduce you to someone else. On a rainy afternoon not long ago I had tea with one of America's best-known educational leaders. Now in her late sixties she is a strikingly handsome woman, bright, witty, in strong command of virtually any public moment. She knows I know she is a lesbian. This permits us to have a certain closeness in discussing gay issues, but always at arm's length. She simply cannot ever share her own story. She still talks about gay people as "them," not "us." In my view, she resents what she perceives as the vulnerability of being a lesbian. It appears as an unfortunate loose link in the armor she wishes to wear before the world.

Beneath her façade of power, I look at a small child— frightened, insecure, desperately in need of tenderness and love—of whom I'm very fond. From her point of view, she has struggled for years to reach the top of her profession. She continues to regard her lesbianism through the eyes of the culture in which she grew up. So she beholds clashing images of social nonrespectability, theological sin, and psychological sickness. Living in the isolation of an ivory tower, she relates neither to the burgeoning gay liberation movement nor to those individual lesbians and gay men with whom she comes in frequent contact. With me she lets down her drawbridge an inch because we're old friends, and, given my involvement in gay issues, it would seem absurd to play a game of total untruth. But the warm companionship and joys of a lesbian or gay extended family remain as much a mystery to her as the Sphinx.

In contrast, I remember an older lesbian who was out of the closet while I was still entrenched in its dark shadows. I was a graduate seminary student preparing for ordination. The church appeared to be, from my vantage point, a wall-to-wall closet case. This not unnaturally made me feel insecure, frightened, threatened, and the loneliest person in the world.

My friend Jean, a healthy, happy, secure lesbian who was an older woman, reached out to me. She took me by the scruff of the neck and decided to help. Grateful, I knew I needed it. She was a genuine friend who understood not only that I was gay, but also that I could not share this information with her. I was still too mired in the homophobia that surrounded me everywhere. She opened her home to me. This was a godsend because it brought me into an ambience of warmth and gentleness, beauty, and hospitality. Always she seemed to have time (in her extraordinarily busy life) to let me express myself and hear me out to the extent that I was able to communicate. We shared ideas, aspirations, fears, laughter.

I had no idea at the time, though I know now, that Jean made me a member of her extended family. Jean walked a mile with me. What did she teach me? That if I grasped the meaning of this, I could return the favor by walking a mile with someone else in need.

You see, it's inexcusably selfish for older gay men and lesbians to be isolated and immersed in loneliness. Our younger sisters and brothers stand in need of our active participation in their lives and in those public issues that affect us all. They need to hear and share our stories, find out how we've survived with grace. Joining the rest of the gay and lesbian community, and the wider human community as well, we're blessed with the opportunity to get on with the work of remythologizing life. In other words, to proceed with the miracle of living.

My life continues to unfold. Presumably I'll experience other birthdays, bombshells, and parades in my life. I look forward to them. I have few if any regrets; everything that's happened to me has contributed to who I am. And I like myself.

It's an incredible privilege to be part of the revolution of the human spirit that has awakened so many of the world's people including, in America, women, African-Americans, Asian-Americans, Hispanic-Americans, gays and lesbians. I've learned that the struggle for human freedom is never realized, never finished. Each succeeding generation has to become involved in its own ways, make its own sacrifices, accept its own responsibilities for the sake of people's liberation.

Older gay men and lesbians must continue, as long as we are alive, to be active participants in the struggle for human freedom.

CHAPTER 4

Reconciliations

BY
VASHTE DOUBLEX

About the Author: Vashte Doublex is a lesbian feminist living in Northern California. She was born in 1927 in Montreal, Quebec, Canada, where she spent her first nine years. She lived for thirty years in England, growing up through World War II. With her family she emigrated to the United States in 1965. She came out in 1972. Currently she is a social worker providing services to disadvantaged and disabled adults.

Doublex has taught college classes and led workshops on women's issues, including aging and ageism. She was an original thinker for the first Old Lesbians Conference in 1987. She is an artist, a poet, and a writer published in many women's magazines and in *Lesbian Land*. She is currently editor of *We Are VISIBLE*, a newsletter for ageful women in and beyond their second Saturn cycle. Subscribers live throughout the U.S. and Canada. For a sample copy of the publication write PO Box 1494, Mendocino, CA 95460.

λ

"**Y**ou'll get over it." I hear his words faint from Oregon and read arrogance into his twenty-three-year-old voice. It had been two months since I sent the telegram to him. Remembering the content I pushed down the emotions that crowded up, placing the receiver carefully in its cradle. "I hate men! All men!" I yelled into the empty room and burst into tears. "Men are not longer a part of my life."

Even now, eighteen years later, I resist remembering the bitter struggle to get to this point. I really loved my sons—yes, I did and do—and yet my strong political beliefs (the correct ones, of course) pushed me to question every value I had, challenge everything I believed in.

I am grateful for much of that questioning. The women's movement and lesbian feminism have opened my eyes, my mind, my spirit, giving me pride in myself and in other women, allowing me to see what miracles we perform daily. I have come to appreciate our struggles and differences, even the separations and probable reconciliations.

It was the spring of 1970 when it all began. Perhaps a little earlier when I made my decision to go to college, to overcome the no-degree stigma. Being in college, thinking and writing, while at the same time feeling the echoes of women's liberation, was exciting, challenging, and frightening. Exciting and challenging because women were getting together everywhere to form consciousness-raising groups; and in those weekly meetings, often for the first time for some of us, we could give each other full attention, time, and space to talk about our frustrations as women, our hopes and fears. Frightening because something was going to have to change, and it would probably be ourselves.

At that time I lived in a big old rambling house with my husband and children, and it was there that we women met, closing the doors on "the men."

Most of us knew each other from working together at the Center for Human Concerns in the small town where I lived and went to college. It was the time of peace signs, the Beatles, and a general feeling of hope for change and peace. It was shocking for some of us as we began to notice the disparities between the sexes, the many discriminations that profoundly affected us, our opportunities for growth, creativity, everything.

Despite ridicule and resistance from the men, we persisted. Our ages ranged from the teens to the fifties. As far as I knew we were all involved in relationships with men. At that moment in time I neither connected with nor had much inkling of a lesbian world. (I was so uninformed in this regard that when visiting Provincetown with my family I didn't notice that there was, as there still is, a large lesbian and gay population.)

We women were angry. We were angry that we had settled for so little; we were angry that we had not known, that we had not been *allowed* to know what we could ask for and expect. We knew nothing about our bodies; most of us were amazed to find we could examine ourselves and each other and see and know the changes within our own vaginas. We discovered "the myth of the vaginal orgasm." We found we knew nothing about our *her*story, about the great women leaders, inventors, adventurers who had gone before. We knew little about finances, about our worth, including wages for housework or the discrimination in the job market for wages and accessibility. (And still today, women earn fifty-nine cents to the men's dollar!) Yes, we were angry, angry and determined to change ourselves and the world.

The bonding I had established in this group with like-minded women, some my age, was shattered when my husband was transferred to Buffalo, New York. I was not happy about it, but felt compelled to follow him with our family. I found I could continue studying for my degree at the State University of New York at Buffalo. Walking timidly around that huge campus I noticed a smaller building with many young women crowded inside, talking animatedly. I had discovered Women's Studies College, one of two existing at that time, which was about to begin its second year with syllabuses exploring all aspects of women's liberation. When I signed up for one of the twenty sections of the introductory class, Women in Contemporary Society, I had no concept of the revolutionary changes coming my way. Classes were limited to twenty women students, and each class was taught by two women who were part of an undergraduate feminist collective.

It was not long before I was part of that collective, teaching the introductory class. I was forty-five at the time. I was painfully aware of the disparity in age and life experience between myself and the rest of the women, most straight from high school. With this is mind and in an effort to make older women's issues visible, I proposed that I teach a section paying particular attention to the liberation of women as they age.

Very little was written about aging. At our weekly collective meetings ageism was not included among the other isms we analyzed and discussed. But I did get permission to teach a section, the first, especially directed toward the older woman. In *Sisterhood Is Powerful* we found a piece by Zoe Moss about women in their forties, entitled "It Hurts to Be Alive and Obsolete: The Aging Woman." Ruth Herschberger's amusing, informative book, *Adam's Rib* (which has a chapter "What Shall We Do with the Climateric?") and, of course, Susan Sontag's essay, *The Double Standard of Aging*, were the limit of our resources. (In the last few years there has been a rapid expansion of resources on women and aging, far less on growing old as a lesbian or on the pervasiveness and effects of ageism.)

What an exciting time it was, starting a women's center, a self-help clinic, forming a feminist acting troupe, and discovering endless energy and enthusiasm to learn and do more. It was then, before my very eyes, that I saw women coming out, and, in fact, an in-joke at the college was "Who came out last night?" I didn't think it would ever be I, although I had loved my women friends all my adult life.

Through all this, my family life was falling apart. I see now how I had set it up so that it was no longer possible to remain. Asking for wages for housework was the cause of a big rift. I felt a non-person as a wife and mother and only felt alive with women friends, teaching and studying. I became unavailable. I lay in the dark most of the summer of 1972, alone on the bed in the master bedroom with Simone de Beauvoir's *The Second Sex* beside me, mourning the coming loss of my family and all I knew. Dramatic as it sounds now, if I wanted to have a life, I had to leave. I knew of no alternatives.

I found a room in a big house in Buffalo that was filled with students from the French Department. My room was at the top of the building, up dusty stairs and at the end of a long hallway. I called it my "womb." It was the first room of my own. In that tiny eight-by-ten-foot space I continued to lay on the bed staring at an old quilt I had hung on the wall. When I wasn't staring I worked, and most weekends I drove the twenty miles to what had been my home to see the children. Leaving was an agony, the younger ones entreating me not to go and asking "But why?" I answered as best I could about my process, about the pain of not being with them, about women's oppression. They sort of understood, and wanted me to return.

Then my husband filed for divorce and custody of the children still at home. My eldest son had left and was living in Oregon.

Reconciliation seemed unlikely, and that was not the limit or the extent of our separation.

In her 1971 essay *The Compassion Trap*, Margaret Adams pointed out that women find it extremely difficult to accept the short-term expediency of permitting (or even failing to prevent) harm to others, even when the long-term results may be highly beneficial. She comments that when a brave wife walks out of an impossible family set-up and leaves the other spouse to rally resources for the children, her behavior is almost always heavily censured. And if she should turn to women and reject close liaison with men? Small wonder we stay "in our place"!

I refused the compassion trap and made a choice to leave the security of my marriage. I chose to love women and not give my love or energy to men. Just as women needed to discover who they were, men could learn to nurture and give in the ways expected from women. I believed in that possibility.

It's no easy task to come out as a lesbian. It felt especially difficult because the women around me were in their twenties with very different backgrounds. My lover was fourteen years younger. Sometimes I was lonely too for same-age women.

And to leave one's children? I did not know any woman who had done such a thing. It was as aberrant—as unnatural as being a lesbian.

I moved into a flat with my lover. It was one of those long, thin apartments and I loved having a place of my own. The children visited and continued to beg me to return. I worked endlessly, went to political meetings, classes and workshops on feminism and women's oppression. We had a large punching bag hanging in the sitting room. It was canvas stuffed with kitty litter and padded with feather pillows. On it we wrote the name of every person or institution that had ever even slightly offended us, and we beat it often. We bequeathed the punching bag to the next woman tenant when we moved out in search of "Dyke Heaven."

In a paper for one of my classes I wrote:

There can be little doubt that the breakdown of norms of thought and behavior are symptomatic of the prerevolutionary period in which we are living. We know chaos and fragmentation precede change in the struggle for new forms. The struggle is epitomized in women.

As we reach a slow recognition of our oppression, the ways we are become invalid—our clothes, makeup, hairstyles are incorrect; our ways of relating to both men and women must be reevaluated constantly; what we have always done unquestioningly for others is looked at critically; our political thinking is shocked into new channels.

Alienation is felt in many ways, and we have to deal with our inner reaction to that outer hostility. When we attempt to speak out, our words fall into a chilly silence or perhaps our appearance is disapproved. Most men view us with a mixture of anger, distaste, and amusement. Many women we meet feel challenged by our behavior and angry at facing the challenge. Hypersensitive to our environment, as we are trained to be, withdrawal of positive responses can put our very survival in jeopardy; our struggles become a neurosis, our changes deviant. Sisters everywhere are shocked and tranquilized into acquiescence and temporary oblivion when their "deviance" is more than their family and friends can bear. How often do we feel alone in our struggles to find a new form for our undefined de-roled selves?

When I wrote this I did not know the extent to which I would de-role myself, moving in a very short space of time from wife and mother to lesbian separatist, a territory unknown to most women and with severe restrictions on activities women and men consider "normal."

We, my lover and I, decided to leave the university when we witnessed sexism, classism, and racism alive and well within its walls. Even Women's Studies was being co-opted when our classes could no longer be taught by women only. And, of course, homophobia was a given.

Leaving the comparative safety, the structure of the university, I longed to create some order out of the chaos. I wanted guidelines, role models, peers. Where were women who had come out later in life? Where were women who had left their marriage and children? Were there other old lesbians?

No one had talked very much then about lesbian separatism. Black power had modeled separatism for people of color, women's consciousness groups had demonstrated the power of women being together without men to discuss women's oppression. I had witnessed, in a college class of only women, the difference in a woman's ability to respond, speak out, show her strength and vulnerability. In the company of only women, women who had been silent became vocal.

Some lesbians said they wished to withdraw all their energies from men because it was men's domination that kept women down. They said they were lesbian separatists.

The pendulum swung to its farthest point and I said, "Yes, that is what I believe." If women changed surely we could change the world. Withdrawing energy from men and their institutions would bring an end to patriarchy and all the oppressions it spawned. I remembered again Margaret Adams's concept of the "compassion trap"—a trap from which few women escape. I did not realize then the extent to which we are held prisoner to play out socially defined roles, nor did I know my courage in rejecting everything I had known. I believed women would understand as I had, and do what I did.

My lover and I left on a quest for freedom. We wanted to live on lesbian land and secede from the world of men; such were our lofty dreams. We connected with small groups of lesbians on similar quests but found differences in ourselves that prevented the dream from materializing. We were only beginning to understand the implications of class and race and their insidious effects on our lives. There was no thought of ageism, ableism or any of the other isms we have since identified. Our attention focused on ourselves as women and how we could be powerful and fully ourselves. As a woman approaching fifty, I certainly had no idea what my full self was.

We connected with a collective in Boston whose leader was so politically correct that other members lived in fear of her critical eye and tongue.

The correct attire was baggy pants, boots, and flannel shirts with short, unstyled hair, no makeup or jewelry. At that time an article was circulating on the politics of being ugly, and the collective saw the value of making ourselves as unattractive as possible (in the stereotypically defined sense) so we would not attract the attention of men. The assumption was that men were attracted to "pretty" women. However, women dressed as we did evoked plenty of attention of the negative kind. We definitely did not look the way a woman is supposed to look. I barely recognized the woman who stared back at me when I looked in a mirror—an activity not encouraged. Behind the bravado I saw fear lurking.

At that time my lover and I were once again without guidelines. Our hopes of creating a woman-only life had not materialized, and I now see how I clutched at rigidity as if it would frame a new world for me. We did not live with the Boston collective, but had frequent meetings with them confronting classism and racism within ourselves and each other. Our longing to be immediately rid of long-held limiting beliefs and prejudices was admirable, our methods sometimes cruel and thoughtless.

The collective could not, of course, condone any relationship with male family members, and I silently nursed in my heart the caring I had for my sons. How could I just stop loving them? It had been hard enough being out of touch for several months. None of the women in this collective had been married or had children; all were many years younger than I.

The crisis came when my eldest son called me and wanted to visit. Without thinking of the consequences I agreed, then in a panic realized I had compromised my commitment to lesbian separatism.

Here are excerpts from the letter I wrote to the collective that encapsulated the tensions, pain, and struggles of that period:

> *What I want to write to you about is this. A week ago I had a call from my eldest son that he was coming East and he asked if he could visit me for a few days. I said yes. Why can't I just separate from him? I haven't seen him for two years, he is twenty-three, he knows I'm a lesbian. When I last spoke to him I was angry with men, but didn't call myself a Lesbian Separatist. We haven't corresponded since I*

saw him two years ago. He left home before I left my husband and told me he believed that I should do whatever was best for me even if it meant leaving. I know he is a man, but ... can you understand? It's hard, sometimes it feels impossible, to let go of this one "person" who has received so much of my love and energy and who has given in return. He even looks like me. Perhaps I do not yet trust in a Lesbian Separatist Community. I have a fear of being alone, I suppose. I want to be really strong about a decision and respect myself, my politics, and you.

My subsequent meeting with the collective was dominated by the leader's ironclad decision: no men in our lives, no exceptions. The next day I sent a telegram to my son: "Cannot meet you or see you. My changes exclude you males." Two months later I picked up the phone and it was my son. "You'll get over it!" he said. I could not believe he might be right.

Eventually I made a painful break from the collective when I realized I had exchanged one form of domination for another. But I continued to hold the belief that separatism would be the catalyst to create liberation for all women.

Time and mores change. Looking back I am ashamed of my judgmental attitudes, especially toward women who did not come up to what I considered the politically correct standard. What happened to kindness, ordinary caring? In her book *Animal Dreams* Barbara Kingsolver writes, "It's hard to give away much when you're the subject of widespread disapproval and your heart is leaking from puncture wounds."

I missed my family and I was lonely for peers, too; for lesbians my age. In November 1978 I left the East Coast on a pilgrimage to the West, searching. I was delighted, enchanted to connect with several old lesbians my age, one even a little older; a phenomenon.

She and I were walking along the beautiful California coast one morning. The sun glinted on the thousands of cobwebs crisscrossing the meadow behind us as we talked of aging, of creating our own reality. She told me about Jane Roberts's book *The Nature of Personal Reality*, and how it was changing her life. The book was about beliefs and how they become truths for us—like the belief that women are inferior to men is not a truth but has become so to many men and women. The conversation turned to our convictions around separatism and the pain I felt without my family in my life. "If you really want to reconnect with your family, your sons, why don't you? What's stopping you?" she asked. I began to see the possibility that I could change my beliefs and not compromise myself. She and I were separatists and we were both old lesbians. I wanted to pay attention. The ice began to melt around my heart. I believe it was the warmth, the comfort of that heart-touch with a lesbian of my years who understood without long explanations, that began the thaw, allowed the reopening.

I wrote to my eldest son, "You said I'd get over it and I was very angry at the time, but you were right and, in fact, it's happening. Much of the anger and pain has gone away as I've become stronger and I no longer want to be separate from you or the rest of the family." A few weeks later he called me and said of course he was pleased to hear from me. He was so matter-of-fact, even wanted me to meet his girlfriend who was a feminist.

Slowly but joyously I rebonded with him and then with the rest of my family. We entered a new phase of friendship and growth, an opportunity to be allies for each other.

Quickly I moved to California to recreate bonds with old lesbians. The disconnection I felt began to diminish as I met women my age and older, some of whose life process through the women's movement had been similar to my own.

In *Ageism in the Lesbian Community*, Baba Copper wrote:

As with naming sexism in the early 1960s the first problem is establishing one's legitimacy, despite the voices which contradict. Whenever an old woman complains of ageism in a gathering of women, there are inevitably those in their late forties for whom it is important to deny the observation. I believe that ageism does not result from fear or envy of the accumulated experience of an elder, nor is it the reflection of some primal response to time toward death, despite the repeated use of these cliches in the apologies of the young. These rationalizations of prejudice, like so many raised in defense of sexism, use their kernel of truth as a diversion. Ageism exists because it rearranges power between women. It robs old lesbians of their rightful place of respect and social equality. With all the strength of self-fulfilling prophecy, it shapes the lives of all lesbians, even the most self-defined and self-confident.... It should be clear to all lesbians that ageism distracts us from the pursuit of our essential Self, the very identity which lesbianism makes possible.

Confronting sexism separated me from my family until I found that part of my lost essential Self. It also separated me from same-age peers and any acknowledgment or validation of what it was to be a woman, a lesbian aging.

I know I am grateful to long-lived friends and my lover, and for feeling a part of a community of old lesbians. I see the importance of and am thankful for an organization like Golden Threads that offers opportunities for connection, friendship and more with old women; and for magazines like

Broomstick and *We Are VISIBLE* for creating and maintaining a network among us. Those of us who attended the first Old Lesbian Conference in 1987 will never forget how deeply touched we were by each others' company. There, with pride, we came out as *old* lesbians. We dared to separate and require that a lesbian be sixty to attend.

I believe there is a place for being separate when that option strengthens and empowers us. The self and group strength created in being with one's own kind can be a catalyst for reconciliation and the unity and harmony most of us long for.

There is a place for women, for lesbians, for old lesbians, and any oppressed group to choose to be with each other only. I appreciate all times and places in which I can be with my sisters with one less oppression to cope with.

I am reconciled to the contradiction of being separate and together. I know that seemingly impossible rifts can be bridged. It gives me hope for the future. It healed the puncture wounds in my heart.

CHAPTER 5

At the Edge of Old Age

BY

MARCIA FREEDMAN

About the Author: In 1967 Marcia Freedman left the United States for Israel where she taught philosophy at Haifa University. There she was one of the founders and leaders of the Israeli feminist movement. In 1973 she was elected to the Israeli Knesset and served until 1977. She was a lone voice for women's issues in that body, raising concerns that had never been spoken of publicly in Israel before: violence against women, rape, incest, teenage prostitution. She also introduced legislation that reformed the country's highly restrictive abortion law. She was an active member of the Israeli peace movement, championing a two-state solution to the Israeli-Palestinian conflict as well as the civil rights of political dissidents and the human rights of Palestinians under occupation.

After her term in the Knesset, she helped pioneer a network of services for women, including Israel's first shelter for battered women, women's centers, rape crisis centers, and a national magazine.

Returning to the United States in 1981, Freedman was a founder of and partner in the Women's Computer Literacy Project. Since 1985 she has been director of marketing and public information for the American Society on Aging and is ASA's liaison to its Task Force on Lesbian and Gay Aging Issues. She is the author of *Exile in the Promised Land* (Firebrand Books, 1991), a memoir of her years in Israel, along with a number of articles and reviews.

───────────────── λ ─────────────────

Two months ago my mother, at age eighty-four, died. She lived in California, not far from me, for the last three years of her life, and I was her caregiver. During the last several months I was her active caregiver. The months preceding and following her death have been another stage in the journey of my own aging. And though it is surely too early to understand the evolution, I will try.

My mother and I never had an easy relationship. Most of my life has been dedicated to being whatever I perceived she was not. She would not have been in California at all had she not come for a visit for her eightieth birthday and suffered a heart attack that left her too frail to return home to what had been her life. So she took an apartment in a retirement community—believing, at first, that all that was left was to linger there until she died.

She did not do that. Instead she turned those last few years into a grand adventure of her own. She had a lover, younger than she by seven years. She studied Yoga and Tai Chi. She learned to play bridge. She had side bets going on the bingo game and found a congenial group for the cocktail hour. She organized the other residents to complain and make demands of the management whenever things didn't please them. "If there's one thing I've learned from your father and you," she told me, "it's how to organize." She became the active center of that retirement community, someone who made others' lives larger and fuller. Until her last day, when she walked with great difficulty and could maintain an activity only for an hour or so without tiring, she was a ball of hot energy that filled all the space available to her. I watched all she did and was with amazement and admiration. I learned from her during those years that the physical body would be what it is, but the spirit could be anything one wished.

Six months ago she was diagnosed with metastatic cancer, already spread to her lungs. I knew then I didn't have much time left with her, and I understood that I would be her primary and sometimes sole caregiver. As such, especially when her needs grew more imperative and the crises developed with increasing frequency, and most especially as the end was in sight, I was challenged in ways I had not been challenged before. My mother, by definition, was the one who was supposed to give to me, to care for me. I had to let go of my anger and disappointment about the many ways she had failed me. I had to find my way toward being able to not fail her. Our roles reversed, and, as I mothered my mother, I found my heart opening to her as it had not been open most of my life.

I was her guide and her advocate in all the painful complexity of end-of-life treatment decisions. I educated her about living wills and durable powers of attorney, and I watched as she hesitated to sign her life over to me with the latter document. It was I who made the final decision not to treat the latest condition that would kill her. It was I who had to tell her half an hour before she died that there was no more treatment possible, no postponement of her date with death. Each decision, each choice, taught me about how I wanted to die and what I needed to do to prepare for it. Facing my mother's death, for the first time I began to face my own.

Since before she came to California I saw her no more than once a year, I saw her getting older in fast-forward. When she turned seventy-five, I was forty-six. That year I realized, for the first time, that my mother was an old woman. Her step was slow and not very sure. Her heart condition was already well developed. She carried small bottles of nitro with her wherever she went. Walking up a flight of steps, she popped a nitro. Laughing too hard or getting too angry, a nitro, like a tiny white exclamation point, slipped under her tongue. Her hair was entirely white and very thin. Though she tried to hide it with artful hair styles, the pink scalp was embarrassingly visible. Her face wasn't too wrinkled, but her body was; the folds of skin hung from her arms, thighs, stomach. Her breasts, once large and full, lay flat on her chest like deflated balloons.

I studied my mother at seventy-five, knowing that I would look just like her in another thirty years or so. At forty-six, thirty years no longer seemed an unimaginable stretch of time.

What did seem unimaginable was what my life would look like at seventy-five. The only thing I knew for sure was that it would not be like my mother's. She'd married young and stayed married until my father's death. From fifty to sixty she'd worked in the family business, but otherwise had been a full-time and fastidious homemaker. And though my father never made much money, he'd managed to pay premiums on enough life insurance to provide her with financial security. She'd lived in the same neighborhood all her married life and still lived there. She and her friends had been playing cards and mah jong together and meeting for lunch several times a week for more than fifty years. Her life was structured almost exactly as it had been when she was thirty, except that in old age she was free of obligations to care for a husband and children; she was free to be, as she termed it, "selfish" for the first time.

I had given up marriage and heterosexuality ten years earlier. Where I lived and what I did had changed so many times during my adult life that there were no structures naturally in place. I'd remade myself again and again. Facing old age, I knew, would require remaking myself once more.

So, I wondered, how do old lesbians live? How do old feminist activists live? Somehow I couldn't imagine myself at seventy-five organizing yet another project that consumed my energy and paid my rent from month to month. My life at forty-six made no sense whatever when projected into the future. Like many of my friends at the time, I later learned, I began to have visions of myself as a bag lady.

It's not surprising that my first thoughts about aging were financial. I had arrived in California from Israel only a few years earlier and rather broke. I was making my way as the director of a women's project I'd founded, drawing twenty-five thousand dollars a year. There was nothing secure about that income. Of course I had no pension. I had no husband's insurance policy or pension plan to look forward to. It was, I knew, time to rejoin the middle class, and that meant finding a job—one that paid well and steadily. I figured I had, at most, twenty or so years to put my old-age economics together.

I was lucky. It took a long time to find, but the job was in nonprofit management with the American Society on Aging. A steady income, some to spare for savings, and a retirement plan. But, best of all, I would work in a field I had so recently come to understand I was living. I bought a house and, for the first time, understood the comfort of permanence. I bought a new car, the first I'd ever owned; a flashy car that defied practicality. I pictured myself looking like my mother and driving around in a red sports car. It pleased me. And I started to save, the hardest move of all since I'd never before seen any value in having money in the bank.

Once the economics were in place, however, I began to comprehend slowly, very slowly, that aging meant a lot more than financial planning. During my late forties I ended a nine-year relationship with the woman I thought would be my partner into old age. My period began to dry up. Every couple of hours my body would heat to the boiling point, and I, who only rarely perspired, began to sweat profusely, the perspiration dripping down my face, neck, and torso. I was moody, and depressions came and went as they had when I was thirteen. More often than not I had no energy, no vitality. And, most remarkably, I had little or no interest in sex. Everything that was the staple of the essential "I" was fragmenting. I no longer knew who I was.

Each morning, staring at myself in the bathroom mirror, I had to reaccommodate to the image that looked back at me. The picture of myself that I carried around in my mind looked nothing like the image in the mirror. The creped skin under my chin altered the shape of my neck. The lines across my forehead, around my eyes and mouth were deeply etched, and my hair was entirely gray.

It was as though there was no continuity between who I had been and what I was becoming. One day, shopping in a department store, I caught sight of someone wearing an outfit identical to the one I had on. It took a very long moment to realize that I was staring at myself in a full-length mirror.

I was growing into a new body, one that would only distantly resemble the body I'd inhabited for the past two decades. It was a body that would need taking care of if it was going to serve my purposes for the next two or three decades. And even then, I knew with painful clarity, there was only so much I could do. Already my blood pressure was high and I was on medication. My cholesterol was dangerously high, too. I was under medical "supervision" for the first time in my life. I could no longer lift heavy objects, and when I needed help (also for the first time in my life) I had to learn to ask for it without feeling shamed and defeated by my body. My friends and I started our social engagements early, because none of us had much energy after 10:00 P.M.

But I also realized, with a clarity that was not painful, that I was growing into a new identity. About that I could do a lot. I started to write the book I'd been meaning to write for a long time. I began to let go of the social activist role that had begun to feel like an endless repetition of my youth. I became more contemplative. I went into therapy, hoping to shed some of the psychological baggage that had driven my earlier choices. I started to study aikido, not so much for my body as for my soul. Those classes, physically difficult at my age, taught me a great deal about how to be centered in the present moment. They also taught me that learning to be centered and present in the moment would be the great challenge of the last third of my life.

No, the journey into and through old age was not only physical, not only financial. It would be, as the earlier part of my life had rarely been, a very personal spiritual journey of identity that would require finding comfort in solitude and redefining my relationship to others. In the past that relationship had been mainly social, sexual, or political; or, in the lesbian feminist world, sometimes all three at the same time.

I wish I could say more about that, but at this stage I'm still learning. I do understand now that the relationships of my youth and early middle age were either taken for granted or instrumental. They made few demands on me, at least consciously, and when they were over I found it easy to leave them behind. By my late forties I had relinquished all too many connections to earlier parts of life. Today, as I age, I begin to understand the importance of longevity and shared memory. I have learned to treasure honesty and openness in my relationships, whether with lovers, friends, or colleagues. I have begun to develop the ability to tolerate vulnerability. There is a need to pay attention to one's relationship to others, and not just for the sake of getting what one wants from them.

When I celebrated my fiftieth birthday, I did so grandly and with pleasure. There was a party in New York with my oldest friends and family on the East Coast. There was another in Berkeley with my new friends—all women, most lesbians, of many different ages. To all who celebrated that birthday with me I launched myself into the third age. Postmenopausal at last, my energy had returned and I felt a new but certain confidence that no matter what would happen to my body over the years, that energy would be with me. There was more security in that than in the retirement accounts or the house.

I'd been bloodless for two years, but I got a final and unusually heavy period on the day of my birthday. It was, I thought, the Goddess's gift, a surge of estrogen to send me off on this new journey toward the end of my life. I wished for myself only that I would be able to make it consciously, honorably, with zest and in community.

Now, at fifty-five, community is what engages my energy more than anything else. I have had a few brief relationships during these years and, once, for a moment, I even tried living with a lover. But no single person, I know, can provide the answer to the questions that preoccupy me. What will happen to me when I'm old and need to be cared for? What would happen to me tomorrow if the heart attack I'm expecting any minute should occur? Beyond the questions of caring, who will be the peers who age with me and reciprocate this consciously examined process I have begun? I treasure solitude. But I treasure, too, communication and sharing the experience of profoundly inexorable change I am undergoing. It provokes the most primal of fears: fear of decay and eventual death. But it also encourages wisdom. And for that to happen, community is essential.

When my closest friend turned fifty, five women, all fifty plus or minus a year or two, met in a restaurant to celebrate her birthday. We talked about menopause, about hot flashes and memory loss, about aging, about our fears and worries, about "what will happen when ..." we grow old. We were, all of us, veterans of the women's liberation movement. We had learned to live our lives with conscious determination in a community of women. That evening we applied that knowledge. We must, we decided, form a group to talk about all of this. The crepey skin, the medical conditions that afflict us, the fears that assail us in the middle of a night sweat when we think about the future, the fact (we admitted hesitantly) that our memories are not what they used to be.

The birthday celebrant suggested that we call ourselves the Wandering Menstruals. It was a good enough name for the transition, I thought. But if we were to succeed as a group it would evolve. For if we were to succeed, we would meet together once a month for the rest of our lives, and the rest of our lives would soon have little to do with menopause and its aftermath.

There are six lesbians in this group of eight women. We have been meeting monthly for four years. Three or four times a year we rent a vacation home for a weekend. Then, in addition to our regular meeting, we can dance together, hike together, cook for one another, and just pass the time of day. At first we tried to prepare a "topic" of discussion for each meeting, but we soon realized that our ongoing lives, the dailiness of the ways we are aging, was our real subject matter. We are tracking one another's lives.

Though we were hesitant and even diffident with one another at the beginning, we are more and more open—some of us to one another, but each of us to the group as a whole. The only thing we know about the future of this group is that we intend to keep on meeting "forever."

In only four years there have been many changes in our lives. Three relationships have ended. Three of the single lesbians are at the beginnings of what look to be long-term relationships. The woman whose birthday party started it all is struggling with thyroid cancer. She is the same woman who, at the beginning, was in mourning for the death of a lover from breast cancer. One of the women had been through intense traumas with each of her three adult children. My mother died and I've also become single once again. We are finding out how to be there for one another, as a group as well as individuals, through these experiences.

For me, during the past six months, this has seemed a more natural and certainly a more comfortable place to share my bereavement than with most of my immediate family, if only because I share so much more of myself in general with these women than I do with family members.

For each of us, in different ways, the group is a primary commitment. We struggle, with each new turn of events in the life of any one of us, with how to experience that turn as a group, in community. We learn from each new experience—the death of a parent, the suicide attempt of a child, the death of a sibling, the end of a relationship, the onset of a life-threatening illness—how this small community can support and sustain each of us. And each crisis, it seems, deepens the community we share.

No one in this group is under fifty anymore. The oldest are fifty-seven, the youngest fifty-two. Four more years will go by as quickly as the past four have gone, and then the oldest will be more than sixty. And then another four more years will go by, and another and another, and we will, as a group, truly enter into old age. None of us can know what that will be like. The only thing we can know now is that we will begin to find out together. For each of us this group is one way to make sure our lives will not unfold without conscious examination, without shared memory, without a caring community.

There are other groups of women our age that meet in the Bay Area. One began a long time ago coming together around the fact that they share a Buddhist practice and call themselves the Dharma Witches. These women, too, are almost all lesbians. Another group, all lesbians, began only recently, self-defined as a health-care community with a prior commitment to provide care for one another when needed. A fourth group, for want of a better name, is called the Lesbian Neighbors. It meets monthly for a potluck and conversation.

What is it about the lesbian experience that prompts conscious community-building as we age? One reason, I am sure, is that we do not have the institution of marriage to count on seeing us through.

Most everyone in the Wandering Menstruals is partnered now, and the relationships seem solid enough. Solid enough, I say, because we all know that our relationships are unstable. They may last a year, five years or ten years. But the possibility of separation is never very far from our minds. For all of the lesbians in the group the ongoing developments in our relationships are a major part of what we talk about. Not so for the married women. Their relationships are a given in their lives, unlike lesbian relationships which are often contingent on how well or poorly they are doing. I have begun to understand from the group that we lesbians are solitary individuals, even though we are aging and could be expected to cling to our partners to see us through old age and the end of life. We have defined our own lives and will continue to do so. We have made no legal commitments and so feel freer to end a relationship and seek a new beginning. It makes our aging harder, much harder. We don't assume anyone will be there. Who will take care of me "when ..." is one of the central questions of our middle-aged lives. We are in this group not just to explore menopause issues, middle-aging issues, but because we perceive, we know, that unless we have a structured community, we could be in trouble. Big trouble.

Because lesbians live their lives as "deviants" and therefore understand the reality of jeopardy, we make fewer assumptions about anything. This is especially so the older we get, and we have learned over the years and through the usual series of short- or long-lived relationships that the partner of the moment may not be the partner forever. As we reach our fiftieth and sixtieth birthdays, we become aware of the possibility of illness, loss, disability, poverty, loneliness, frailty. It is a frightening realization for women who have learned to be self-reliant that self-reliance won't work forever. We seek, and need to create, communities of the committed—of those who will be there to take care of us when we need to be taken care of.

Although the institution of marriage is changing significantly, the internalized attitudes and assumptions about marriage are slow to adjust to new realities. So it is still that many traditional middle-aged and older women are caught short and thrown into crisis by the death of a spouse or by late-life divorce.

One of the assumptions about marriage is that the relationship is cast in concrete and maintained by millennia of institutional supports. Couples marry in public ceremonies that state "till death do us part." Most traditional married women, I think, never stop to consider the odds that they will survive a full decade, or even two or three, alone. They assume that their financial needs in old age have been taken care of by the fact of their long-lived marriages. This may be true in many cases, but it is untrue in most. Yet there is the assumption of a caring community (that is, husband and children) and a financially secure old age that goes along with the marriage vows. Sometimes it works. Sometimes it doesn't.

There is another reason, I believe, why we middle-aged lesbians actively create intentional communities. It is that we have learned through the years the value and true pleasure of belonging to a community of independent women each creating her own life.

Whether we came out as teenagers or as sixty-year-olds, we have known that part of coming out is a declaration of independence. I will not accept societal norms. I will live according to the choices I make. I will define myself by these choices. I accept my difference and all that it entails. I even rejoice in my difference and all that it entails. For oneself there is enormous excitement, sometimes anxiety, in living a life of existential self-definition. In community there is deep pleasure and sometimes rare joy in coming together to learn about and bond with other women whose experience of a lifetime has been predicated on their individuality.

We have, all of us, known from the beginning that we would have to make our own ways. We have known that we would have to uniquely define ourselves and our relationships: with one another, with our partners of the moment, with our families, with our co-workers, with our neighbors. We have had few predecessors to model ourselves after; a century of closeted lives has ensured that. Without precedents, without models, we have lived with the ultimate existential condition that, really, is every woman's condition. But we have lived with it consciously and not always by choice. That condition is self-definition.

We have also lived with a sense, always conscious, of our vulnerability. We could be fired for our lesbianism. We could be evicted because of our lesbianism. We could be officially branded as deviants and perverts. We could be ostracized for our lesbianism. We could even be killed for our lesbianism. As lesbians, we have lived on the edge of danger, always.

The need for self-definition and the ever-present sense of vulnerability combine to underscore an existential aloneness in the world that no partner, no matter how long-term, can erase. For many lesbian women who are already in old age that has meant enduring an isolation from society that, to me, seems barely tolerable. And yet I know there are millions of women who are doing it with varying degrees of success.

But for those of us who are now just entering the portals of old age there seem to be other options—options we have learned about because we were and are part of the women's movement. That movement grew out of consciousness-raising groups in which we shared our most personal experiences in order to discover the political, social, and psychological structures that oppressed us. These groups were the original cadres of a movement for social change, but they were also the breeding ground for countless individual personal changes. How many of these groups were, or became, predominantly lesbian?

We individually experimented with and changed our lives, and to a large extent modeled new visions of what a woman's life span might encompass. Now, at the edge of old age, I still have no idea at all of what it will look and feel like. How could I? What I am beginning to understand, however, is that old age may well be the next lesbian feminist frontier, and I look forward to having a piece of the action.

CHAPTER 6

Will You Still Love Me When I'm Seventy-Four?

BY
MORRIS KIGHT

About the Author: Morris Kight turned seventy in 1989 with an exhibition of the McCadden Place Collection of posters, prints, paintings, and photographs of movements with which he has been identified: lesbian and gay, Jewish, Chicano/Latino/Hispanic, Black self-determination, feminist, and environmental. He was founder of the Dow Action Committee, which in the 1960s exposed the carcinogenic effects of Agent Orange; founder of the Gay Liberation Front of Los Angeles; co-founder of Christopher Street-West, the Gay and Lesbian Community Services Center; co-founder of Asian/Pacific Lesbian and Gays; and commissioner of Human Relations for the Country of Los Angeles.

From 1937 to 1942 he attempted to integrate the university he attended. Later he joined the NAACP. He has insisted on an integrated board of directors of any activity he has joined. This eventually took him into work with the Southern Conference Educational Fund in Louisville, Kentucky, and into association with the Southern Christian Leadership Conference.

Since 1942 Kight has taken part in special study health-services administration. He has analyzed and written widely on public policy issues, particularly in the areas of civil liberties, civil rights, social service delivery mechanisms, defense budgets, foreign policy, urban renewal, and housing.

He is active on many political fronts. With Howard Fox and others he helped found the Stonewall Democratic Club, was its first president, and remains actively involved with it. In 1978 he became a member of the California State Democratic Central Committee. He is a member of the State Committee on Civil and Human Rights of the Platform Committee as well as a co-chair of the Delegate Selection/Affirmative Action Committee of the California Democratic party.

Morris Kight's accolades include the Eason Monroe Courageous Advocate Award from the American Civil Liberties Union, and the Eleanor Roosevelt Humanitarian Award/Southern California Americans for Democratic Action.

So here we are well into the last decade of the twentieth century and we find growing activism among old/older/senior lesbians and gays, and it's high time for it. How many of us are there? Nobody knows. Certainly a lot of us are around, many of us out of the closet, some of us quite happy, content, and living lives of achievement and satisfaction. Some of us are quite unhappy, physically ill, and living lives of loneliness and despair. Many old folks among us are not out of the closet, and in a time when "outing" has been a major source of discussion, what about that?

It is absolutely necessary to be out of the closet to be happy and fulfilled. Certainly the closet is an ugly place; you can go crazy in there. Many techniques have been developed to be done with the closet; indeed, a whole industry has sprung up to teach us how to get out of the closet and to wind up on the other side with fullness of personality, indeed, achieving gestalt.

What about us old folks and the coming out ritual? Hardly an item of major concern among us. Our personalities are pretty well fixed in place and whether to come out or not is of little consequence. Far larger items of concern.

How, ever, did we wind up with a second generation of out, activist, somewhat unified and socially concerned lesbians and gays? It is a fascinating history and ranks as one of the great success stories of all time.

THE HISTORY

1969 and all that: The state of affairs for lesbian and gay people in 1969 was sick, sad, and sorry. There was an almost total monolith of oppression, exploitation, and repression facing us on every day, and in every way. Let us tick off some of the institutions that were down on us.

THE STATE

The state in all of its manifestations. The famous dictum that the state exists to promote "life, liberty, and the pursuit of happiness" hardly applied to us. State-run institutions engaged in the protection of civil rights not only did not protect us, they often were downright hostile. It was nearly impossible to get a professional license if there was any indication that you might be lesbian or gay. Indeed, it was very nearly impossible to get a license to practice very nearly any trade, except the stereotypical trades of antique dealing, poodle trimming, and hairdressing.

THE POLICE

As an agent of the state, the police treated us as unapprehended, and unconvicted, criminals. There were frequent raids of places of public accommodation. Gay men were arrested in the streets for just being, and raids on our homes and social affairs, without the benefit of search warrants or probable cause, were quite common. It was so bad that gays created an expression for it: "bull horrors." Bull was the underground term for police officers, and horrors was the response on seeing one.

EDUCATION

Schools and libraries had it that we were guilty of abnormal behavior. That was the teaching in all educational institutions, be they university, college, secondary, or elementary schools. Whole chapters in books had us as sick, sinful, deviant, variant, and abnormal. One personality test provided in universities, the Stanford-Binet, included a section to determine masculinity/femininity of men.

NUCLEAR FAMILY

All of us had one, have one, and they treated us as if we were a birth defect, or an inherited characteristic of the less popular side of the family. One family in an eastern state took its son/brother to a state psychiatric facility where electroconvulsive shock therapy was performed on him. This was in 1956. As an added item the staff had the patients waiting on gurneys in the hall while the procedure was done in an operating room with an open double-door. They were thus able to witness the writhing, the convulsions.

THE CHURCH

As an absolute monolith the church treated us as having so little spiritual worth it did not even bother to send missionaries to save us. It sent them for everybody else—all those treated as Gentiles, sinners, reprobate persons or infidels—but not us. The rejection was absolutely shattering to those of us who had strong family/church ties. In Christianity, the books of Leviticus, Corinthians, and Romans came down very hard on us, calling our love "an abomination," another prescribing the death penalty for performing a same-gender sex act.

PSYCHIATRY

In the beginning of this century a brand-new "science" came into existence: psychiatry. While the human mind is a stunningly complex instrument, certainly one that can get out of whack and thus any responsible program of treatment should be applauded, in the case of homosexuals, they lost it. According to psychiatry, "The church declared these people sinful, certainly a declaration by a most imprecise institution; we find them sick." So, we wound up with the most formidable enemy we have ever had. Jacketed, tied, well-groomed "scientists" put us on the sick list, and under that rubric millions lost status. Many of us were lobotomized, many were "treated" with mind-altering drugs, and a stunning number were subjected to electroconvulsive shock therapy.

CAPITALISM

Employers felt that we were suitable only for entry-level work, or froze us in the employment scale at, at best, mid-level employment. Merchants considered us credit risks; property owners often refused to rent to us.

SOCIALISM

With all their high-sounding rhetoric about "the common person," socialists treated us as inferiors, often classed us as suffering from "bourgeois decadence." They had it that all that fat capitalist living was bound to lead to some defect in our character.

OPPRESSION SICKNESS

And, oh! How sad it is to note that we were often our own worst enemies! If everyone you meet treats you as sick, sinful, deviant, variant, inferior, unemployable, or the subject of righteous discrimination, you might very likely internalize some of that alleged inferiority. Thus some of us drank too much, ate too much, had low self-esteem, failed to compete fully in the marketplace and the world of social intercourse. We were often a mess. The closet was a place of great temptation where we often learned to deceive all those we dealt with by pretending to be something we simply were not: heterosexual.

THE REBELLION

In 1969, spurred on by the anti-war movement, black power movement, and the hippie revolution, we finally found it in our best interest to commence a nonviolent revolution. Thus in late 1969 Gay Liberation fronts were created in New York, Berkeley, Los Angeles, San Francisco, and San Jose, California, in that order. During 1970 very nearly three hundred sprang up in the country, and the world has been a far better place for us ever since.

There was a rebellion at a gay bar in Greenwich Village during the last weekend in June 1969 that has taken on absolute mythic proportions. Agents of the Alcoholic Beverage Control Board of New York, accompanied by New York Police Department officers, came into the Stonewall Inn at 59 Christopher Street, presumably to check out the unlicensed nature of the premises. As was their unfortunate habit they spoke derisively of the customers, and at two o'clock in the morning started checking them out and letting them leave one at a time.

When the customers were out on the sidewalk they did not slink guiltily away as had been our habit for centuries. Instead they stayed around to protest, picket, and rally. For three days an action went forth in Sheridan Square, and the event gradually became an important act of resistance for our personal liberation.

It has been called the "commencement of radical lesbian and gay liberation in our country." It was no such thing; it was an important event and one we should honor. We will do so with a worldwide celebration in New York in June 1994 when we celebrate "Stonewall-25."

From 1969 onward we have sought through demonstrations, lawsuits, civil disobedience, conferences, teach-ins, and the foundation of service-delivering organizations, the creation of a movement—and of a community.

We have lobbied the federal, state, and city governments to include us in civil liberties, civil rights, and administrative services. There have been massive reforms in the law to decriminalize our behavior, and to include us in protective procedures.

We have demonstrated against the police, sued them, confronted them, committed civil disobedience against them, and sought civil dialogue and communication with them. While the struggle is not over, vast changes have come about.

The negative textbooks that once taught we were abnormal are long since gone, and some curriculums include us as one more minority to be dealt with and included. Project 10, created in Los Angeles as a specific concern for lesbian and gay students, is being replicated in schools all over the country.

Our families have enjoyed the same massive education everyone else has had and thus are bound to have had a healthy change of attitude about us. A powerful and evergrowing organization, Parents and Friends of Lesbians and Gays, has emerged and constitutes a powerful support group for parents dealing with their children's lesbianism and gayness.

OUR HERITAGE

The weakest link in our chains, however, is dealing with our young/younger/youthful sisters and brothers. It remains our most exasperating problem. Simply it is this: Many new people are born every moment; some are people of color—African-American, Latino/Latina, Asian, Pacific Islander, or Native American—and all things being the same it is foretold that they might very well suffer some exploitation, if not be the victims of genocide. Many of us believe that every tenth of those newborns is one of us, lesbian or gay, but nobody knows that. Not mother or father, the attending medical staff, grandmother or grandfather, uncle or aunt. No one knows. Before that new person is three, maybe four, he or she knows, however, and being a quick learner has heard that it is not a good thing to talk about, to discuss, lest he or she be evicted from the home, sent out for cure or punished, or treated in a special—meaning inferior—way.

So the first fourteen, fifteen, sixteen, seventeen years are a time of denial, or anonymity; of hiding. And thus we lesbian and gay folks are cursed to live the first part of our lives in what amounts to quiet desperation.

The church is perhaps where we have made the largest single advance. Our community has created its own Christian outreach, The Metropolitan Community Churches, now a worldwide activity. Dignity is a Roman Catholic organization to provide support and succor for lesbian and gay members of that faith. Beth Chadashim, founded in Los Angeles in 1971, was history's first-ever outreach to lesbian and gay Jews and was the replicable force for many such groups. Caucuses exist in very nearly every denomination, and many churches have a specific program for lesbian and gay members.

The psychiatric profession has benefited from our educational efforts. We carried out an intensive four-year effort to reach it with the essential message that it had committed an incorrect diagnosis that had made us the victims of genocide. In the summer of 1973 when *Diagnostic and Statistical Manual III* was published, we were omitted from the sick list.

Capitalism and socialism have done a near-total turnaround in their attitudes toward us. Capitalism has found that dollar bills have no sexual orientation, and is increasingly fighting for those bills. Lesbian and gay groups are commencing to appear in what only a short time ago was the Eastern Bloc, and now President Boris Yeltsen of Russia has proposed that gay men's acts of love be dropped from the criminal code.

Yet our greatest victory has been over self. Before 1971 ended millions of us had come out and quickly begun to abandon any notion of our alleged inferiority.

We have created some stunningly powerful institutions that have a lasting quality. In New York we have Heritage of Pride, the group that stages an annual celebration of the Stonewall Uprising. In Los Angeles, the last Sunday in each

June sees a massive parade and festival attended by 350,000 people. Both events first occurred on Sunday, June 28, 1970, as a Commencement or New Way.

In Los Angeles is the magnificent Gay and Lesbian Community Services Center founded in spring 1971. It is the largest lesbian and gay social service agency in the world, has the largest staff, the most building space, the largest budget. It is the model for many throughout this country and is now beginning to be replicated in other countries.

So we are not who we used to be. We are a changed, and changing, people. Much work needs to be done to continue our agenda, the road map has been developed, and guides exist to lead us onward.

Now we come to the needs of old/older/senior lesbians and gays. Why the word? I love the word "old." It's so clear, so short, so definitive, and I think it has great dignity attached to it. I use it in hope of overcoming ageism.

"Older" is a genteel euphemism that overcomes so many people's resistance to dealing with their aging. Since a child born yesterday is a day older today, this little witticism gives everyone a chance to be a part of us without proclaiming that he or she is actually old. Senior is a popular appellation that contains precious little dignity. It does have one creative value: It entitles us to discounts.

So what do we old lesbian and gay folks need, and want?

SECURITY/SAFETY

Certainly those are goals everyone desires but violence is a way of life in our world. We must learn how to cope with it. Old folks, of any gender or sexual orientation, are being bashed, and elder abuse is a major problem. Perhaps it always was, but now it's out in the open. We can do so many things to protect ourselves: carry only small amounts of ready cash; keep ready cash and credit cards, along with personal identification, close to our bodies where it's not reachable by strangers; be careful about walking in the streets at night.

Security means much more than just physical security, however. If we older folks wish to be really helpful we can encourage our young/younger peers to plan right now for their old age: to get an excellent education, to develop managerial skills, and yes, to enter the professions. Doctors, lawyers, dentists, and psychiatrists make a lot more money than equipment installers. So go for the top. Those of us well into our years should probably not count on making a fortune late in life, but if you can figure it out, go for it!

SEARCHING/SERENDIPITY

Dare to socialize, consort, get about, attend lectures, concerts, festivals, the works. Our society produces more events than can possibly be attended. Learn to use the events calendar, call around, ask if there is any kind of special deal for oldsters. Then go! And when there, get acquainted. Many of these events are free. I know a group of seniors who go to the Hollywood Bowl during the day in the summer to hear and watch rehearsals. They are out-of-doors, in a safe and pleasant environment, watching great art being constructed right before their eyes. And it's free. The artists are pleased to have a live, and enthusiastic, audience. Everyone loves applause.

SATISFACTION

A satisfied and fulfilled life is so much better than a barren and incomplete one. Think of all the things that make you happy—and do them. Volunteer at some place where service to people is an important part of the program. A quiet hobby I have pursued for fifty years is going into the book sections of thrift shops, yard sales, and charity auctions to buy back the library books. They cost the body politic a great deal, and why are they in the discard bin? Thoughtless people. Someone moves and leaves books behind, someone loses control, or ...? Thus I package and send them; the thoughtful United States Postal Service has a book rate that is dirt cheap. I am careful to not give a name; the only thanks I want is the feeling of just doing.

SEXUAL SATISFACTION

Now we come to a very delicate subject: sexual satisfaction. There are great barriers to sexual activity for old people, especially gay males. Ours has been a youth-oriented community. Sexual activity has been considered the ultimate achievement and satiety. Much of this stems from the insecurity of the preliberation era when sex was often furtive, often dangerous, and one never knew when arrest or exposure would befall. So we got it in a hurry, and youth was a totally desirable characteristic. Now twenty-three years into our personal liberation it is time to pull back, to look at it as it is, and then to start doing something to promote intergeneration sexual activity. Body-consciousness sessions, sensitivity training, and just downright adventure: Dare to do it, and enjoy it.

THE SURROUND

Our homes, offices, and work environments can be made lovely, inspiring, satisfying, filled with vistas. Plant shrubs and trees in the garden. If there is no garden, place plants on the windowsill. Fill our shelves with readable and enjoyable reading matter. Books can be very inexpensive. We can buy good ones, even great ones, in thrift shops, at yard sales, at community charity auctions. Since books are a hard sell at some events, if you indicate interest they'll let you set your own price. Select, care for, and love animals. Dogs and cats have spent millenniums grooming themselves to be our companions. I have a fantasy that it all started with the emergence of fire. Cats and dogs had to survive in the forest just like the rest. So here they stood out in the dark and cold, and saw us with fires, with warmth and comfort. They saw us having a great time of it, and being innately smart, they said, "That seems to beat the hell out of this hard row, so let's join 'em." To do that they had to make themselves desirable, attractive, useful. Thus they purr—the wagging tail, the I-never-saw-a-lap-I-did-not-want-to-sit-on attitude—and thus there they are, loving, nonjudgmental, and loyal friends. Enjoy!

As for beauty, it is so fulfilling, so important in our expansion of consciousness, our lives, our satisfaction, that I urge all of us to collect the most interesting furniture, utensils, and art works we can find. Posters are the poor person's art. They cost very little, are in constant production, and if you are interested in appreciated value, they can become quite valuable. Item: In 1955 Pablo Picasso created his famous poster with the dove of peace bearing the olive branch for an international peace conference. One of these posters sold at auction in 1980 for fifteen thousand dollars. That is why I have created the McCadden Place Collection. It comprises fifteen hundred pieces on exhibit in the compound at McCadden Place, with possibly two thousand more stored in cabinets awaiting cataloging, appraisal, and a decision as to what to do with them. The poster is the absolute heart and soul of the collection.

HEALTH

Perhaps our greatest concern is for our health. Before the liberation many of us abused ourselves—drank too much, developed diminished self-esteem, did not achieve in the marketplace sufficiently to live in style and grace—and thus our collective health is of urgent concern to some of us. Many things can be done to improve our health, and let's commence with holistic care. If you abuse alcohol or drugs, cut it out. There are ways to do that. Ask around. If you eat a lot of sweets and fats, think about fresh fruit, vegetables, and tofu.

Hospital and doctor bills are a huge, out-of-control item. In 1964 President Lyndon Johnson urged upon the Congress the passage of Medicare legislation, certainly one of history's great social advances. Use it, you've earned it. Shop around, ask who does this and who does that. Go for the best, and learn to challenge. Ask for a second opinion, particularly if surgery is recommended.

But perhaps the most important part of our health development and maintenance is our thought processes and uses of energy. Think positively, think creatively. There are problems in the world and they need to be solved. Be part of the solution, but in doing so believe in the innate possibilities of the human potential. Given a fair field, access to lots of information and the ability to assimilate facts, each of us can be an agent of social change.

THE END OF TIME

Death must come at last to one and all. So prepare for it. Not morbidly, but with the joy of achievement. However much or little you might have, make a will; and do it today. Make it as detailed as reality dictates. Write it all out, making clear who is to get what, and what you want done at your death. Write it in longhand if you wish. Then take the whole thing to an attorney and consult him or her about it. There are attorneys who do this *pro bono*, as well as legal clinics, if money is an issue for you. But if you keep it in longhand, do have two people witness it. However much or little you might have, give a lot of thought to the most creative use for it. The new generation of lesbian and gay people need not go through the pauperite horror many of us experienced before liberation.

We have spun off many institutions and they all need support. Certainly not all of them are attractive to all of us, but somebody somewhere loves them, and ought to support them. So leave money to the institution of your choice.

If you are totally at home with your natal family, if you love and like each other, consider them for bequests. But our community could surely use the gratuity. Item: A small religious group recently got a four thousand dollars bequest. The board of directors met and decided, with much love aforethought, to use half of it to pay off its total indebtedness, and agreed to use the remaining half for educational outreach. All this in the donor's memory.

I have written long and with some sense of the history of what we've been through.

Let me become very personal and spell out my own agenda to the year 1999: I will be eighty that year, and am having the time of my life planning for the decade.

The McCadden Place Collection has grown very large, and now it possesses me. I have given it to the board of directors of the Gay and Lesbian Community Services Center. The Center has a corporate structure to absorb it and I am working with the board to develop a program of exhibitions, traveling shows, and the study of art collecting. I hope there will soon be a paid professional staff: a curator, gallery specialists and art educators.

Stonewall-25: I went to Fort Lauderdale, Florida, in October 1985 to present a six-page position paper to the International Association of Gay and Lesbian Pride, Inc. In it I proposed that we all gather in New York in June 1994 to celebrate the Stonewall Uprising. I urged us to get together. We can have as many events as we have the imagination and energy to formulate. Our great opportunity in this is to internationalize our movement. We say we are everywhere, and we know that to be absolutely true. Now let's show it! Can you imagine the joy of it, millions marching down Fifth

Avenue with the banners of all continents, all nations, all cultures? I can hardly wait.

After Stonewall-25 I want to write two books. One would be an expansion on this chapter. Who we were, what it was like, where all this hatred for us came from, how some of us resisted it and survived. And then in 1969 a grass roots, nearly spontaneous nonviolent revolution came into being. We have organized, educated, moved, challenged, changed and been changed, and thus we are not who we used to be. We are somebody else—and what a joyous day it is!

A second book would be on how much better we could live our lives than the way we do. I would emphasize unity, cooperative effort, the building of chosen family, care for our health and the environment, and faith.

CHAPTER 7

Old and Gay

BY
ARLENE KOCHMAN

About the Author: Arlene Kochman is currently a D.S.W. candidate in Fordham University's School of Social Welfare. She earned her M.S.W. at Adelphi University in 1966 and her M.S. in Education at New York University in 1960. She is a certified social worker in New York State.

Kochman has worked for SAGE—Senior Action in a Gay Environment, Inc.—since 1985. She has served as its executive director since 1990. SAGE is the only nationwide social service agency serving gay and lesbian elderly. As administrative head of its service delivery system, Kochman provides professional leadership and daily direction to the service personnel (staff, interns, and volunteers) as they work toward short-, intermediate-, and long-term service goals and objectives for SAGE's clients. She is charged with program planning and development, administration, and supervision of SAGE's homebound program for the frail and elderly (which is under contract with New York City's Department for the Aging), design and implementation of an annual survey of service recipient's characteristics, consultation with the board of directors' Long Range Planning Committee for the design and execution of a needs-assessment instrument, and coordination and training of service volunteers active in SAGE's public education and outreach programs.

In 1989 she developed an AIDS and the Elderly Program that has become known throughout the nation. Before going to SAGE, Kochman served as National Inspector for Family Treatment, Ministry of Labor and Social Affairs, Department of Services to the Individual and Family for the government of Israel. This position included designing and developing government policy on all aspects of family treatment for nationwide dissemination as well as training and supervising of regional directors. She also replicated PACT, a family-based program she had designed in the United States, and compiled and implemented a group work curriculum.

Kochman has published and given presentations on gay and lesbian aging and on HIV/AIDS issues at local, regional, and national conferences of such organizations as the National Council on Aging, American Society on Aging, State Association of Gerontological Educators, New York State Council for Family Relations, and the National Association of Social Workers.

In the early 1970s our society began to realize the great cultural wealth offered by its older adults. With the aging of America came a sense of responsibility to address our older Americans' special needs and issues so they might continue to lead full lives. This awareness, however, did not (and even now does not) always recognize that there is a gay and lesbian group within the older population.

Yet this group has contributed equally to our culture and society and also has a long history and culture of its own. This invisible minority of older gay men and lesbians has been relegated to a land where they are never seen or heard from. Like the Amer-Asian child of the conflict in Southeast Asia, the older homosexual is not wanted by either side—by the elderly or the younger homosexuals. Can society really believe that homosexuals self-destruct at age forty? Have the gay male and lesbian communities been so oblivious to their own futures that they have succeeded in excluding older persons from their bars, their organizations, their literature, and their social activism? Gay and lesbian seniors do exist; we are in every community, every workplace, every profession, and every family constellation. What keeps us invisible?

The prejudices against those with affectional preferences for their own sex remains so strong that most of society does not provide a comfortable or comforting ambiance for the older gay man or lesbian. The history of social harassment is such that many cannot bring themselves to trust fully even the increasingly numerous broad-minded members of the heterosexual world.

The gay or lesbian senior shares the same concerns of all elder citizens. We are concerned about health care, transportation, satisfactory housing, availability of jobs and job training, retirement, and the opportunity to make meaningful use of our leisure time through recreational pursuits. We are also concerned with our body changes, our loss of friends, our lack of consistent mobility, and with being old in a youth-oriented society.

We know that most of us do not fit into the stereotype the heterosexual world has fashioned for us. We do not all reside in the gay area of Greenwich Village or San Francisco where they have chosen to ghettoize us. We know we are diverse members of society and of our own subculture. We are each unique in appearance and in lifestyle. Many of us have married; some of us are parents and grandparents. Some enjoy long-term relationships, others live alone. Some are part of the healthy well and independent elderly population, others are part of the minimally or moderately impaired population, still others need institutional care. Some of us are well connected to supportive systems, others are alone or have outlived key people in our lives. Whoever we are, however, and wherever or with whomever we choose to live, many of us still choose to remain invisible.

The choice of invisibility should not be scoffed at by the younger activist members of the gay and lesbian community; it should be understood in the context of our history and experience in this society. Our invisibility is related to fear, which is based on past and present societal prejudices. When many of us were growing up in America we were labeled sick by the medical profession, immoral by the clergy, unfit by the military, menacing by the police. We lived with the fear of losing jobs, homes, friends, and family. Though the gay and lesbian community has come a long way concerning civil rights, living with and often internalizing constant homophobia is difficult to overcome.

Today, at the dawn of a new era, we are faced with AIDS—which further promotes homophobia. We are overwhelmed by legislative acts voted in Colorado and in Tampa, Florida, that say our rights do not have to be protected. What to do: Come out and be strong in numbers? Stay invisible and often isolated and lonely? Make a choice?

Or indeed make no choice? The heterosexual older person does not have to make a choice to live as a total human being, to declare who she or he is and with whom she or he makes a life. We can make a choice or not; but it is important to us as human beings in the golden years of our lives that we have a choice.

And we do. We can declare who we are to our friends and families and peers, or we can not. We can remain who we are and build up our own support networks so we can form our own groups of safety and security, or we cannot. A model for this positive direction is SAGE, Senior Action in a Gay Environment, Inc. SAGE members belong and maintain a safe space for ourselves. We empower ourselves by being part of an organization that represents who we are and that stands up for us. We may choose to belong, but not stand out or up front. That choice is ours, and choice makes us strong.

In order to make choices we must also raise questions that are crucial, or at least concern us:

▼ *Am I Normal?* You are who you are. Be proud of yourself. If you know your sexual orientation lies within your own gender, accept that fact, and accept yourself for who you are. Know that more than 10 percent of the population are also a part of the gay and lesbian population.

▼ *Are We a Family?* You have, with your lover, created a unit, a nuclear family. Your family system—living together, sharing and loving one another—is as good as, if not better than, any other family system. With your gay and lesbian close friends you have created a supportive and nurturing extended family that is all the more functional because it is a family of choice and preference.

▼ *What About Loneliness and Isolation?* Like any elderly person who is no longer in the work force, you must create your own socialization space. Think about where you live: Is it accessible to places and people? Have you built up relationships in your life? Do not be afraid to seek out the gay and lesbian bookstores and centers to see if there is a group over forty or fifty; if there is no such group (and there probably isn't), start one!

We at SAGE have just begun to help communities across the United States and in Canada begin to set up senior gay and lesbian activities. Don't sit back and wait. Investigate your community and create something yourself. Volunteer in your community: Senior volunteers are needed in hospitals and other organizations, gay and straight, particularly among groups working in AIDS. Sharing ourselves really does enhance our self-esteem. It's gratifying; it enables us to have a destination, a purpose, a sense of giving to others. Being a role model to gay and lesbian people coming up and out can make you feel really good about yourself. After all, we are the survivors. We lived, loved, worked, and cared for ourselves under the most prejudicial circumstances. We should be proud.

Aging is easier when we form social systems in our lives. If through the years we have utilized our inner resources and surrounded ourselves with support systems, we are ahead of the game. If we have utilized our psychic energy to live, love, and support ourselves but have not developed outside support systems, we can still do so. If we have lost the systems that have kept us going throughout our lives we need to reach out for new ones. No one comes to you: You must mobilize yourself, at least to a minimal degree, and say, "I need help. I need to talk to someone like me, I need to know that I am not the only gay or lesbian person over fifty in this world."

This networking responsibility is not yours alone, but the first step may well be. Take that step. Life can be good at any age if you you take some control over it!

CHAPTER 8
Old Lesbians Seizing the Moment, Changing Their World

BY
SHARON M. RAPHAEL
& MINA K. ROBINSON MEYER

About the Authors: Sharon M. Raphael earned her Ph.D. in sociology at Case-Western Reserve University in Cleveland, Ohio, in 1974. She earned a B.A. at Hiram College in 1963 and an M.A. in sociology at Western Reserve University in 1965. She taught at the University of Akron (1965-66), Kent State University (1966-67), and Cleveland State University (1968-70). After moving to Los Angeles in 1970 she began work on her doctoral dissertation, *Coming Out: The Emergence of the Movement Lesbian* (1974), a pioneering study of a group of lesbians who came out together in the early years of gay liberation in Los Angeles.

In 1970 she accepted a teaching position in the Sociology Department at California State University, Dominguez Hills, in Carson, California; she is now a full professor there. Founder of the M.A. program in gerontology at CSUDH and coordinator of that program for the past fifteen years, she recently completed two years as chair of the Department of Sociology. In addition, she is faculty adviser to the campus Gay and Lesbian Student Union, founder of and adviser to the Older Adult Center, and has served on the University's AIDS Task Force.

Raphael co-founded the National Association for Lesbian and Gay Gerontology in 1978. She has published and given numerous papers in the area of lesbian and gay studies, primarily on lesbian and gay aging issues, and has organized and moderated many symposiums and panels at professional gerontology meetings on lesbian and gay aging topics. Active in the gay and lesbian community in Los Angeles since 1971, she is a founding member of and consultant to the AIDS HealthCare Foundation, a member of Lambda Democratic Club in Long Beach, and a board member of Long Beach Area Citizens Involved (LBACI).

Honors include the Award of Merit for Outstanding Achievement for work in Lesbian and Gay Aging (1981), the Gerontologist's Award for Contributions to Research and Education (1983) from the National Association for Lesbian and Gay Gerontology, and Christopher Street West's Steve Berman Award for Outstanding Service to the Los Angeles Lesbian and Gay Community. She lives with her life mate and coauthor, Mina Robinson Meyer, and enjoys the very full life of activism, work, and play they have created together.

....

Mina Robinson Meyer is a human relations commissioner for the city of Long Beach, California, where she lives with her life mate and coauthor, Sharon Raphael. She serves as a consultant to AIDS HealthCare Foundation, a pioneering organization of which she is a founder. She has received the Award of Merit for Outstanding Achievement for work in Lesbian and Gay Aging (1981) and the Gerontologist's Award for Contributions to Research and Education (1983) from the National Association for Lesbian and Gay Gerontology, an organization she also helped found (1978).

Other honors include Director Emeritus, Gay and Lesbian Community Services Center (1973); Christopher Street West's Steve Berman Award for Outstanding Service to the Los Angeles Lesbian and Gay Community (1987); and the Heart of Gold Award, AIDS Hall of Fame, L.A. AIDS Hospice (1987). She was chosen as one of the Advocate 400, a group of four hundred lesbians and gay men from across the nation being honored as leaders in the fight for gay and lesbian liberation by *The Advocate* (1984), and as one of ten Quintessential Angelenos by *L.A. Weekly* (1989).

Robinson Meyer has been presenting papers at professional meetings primarily in the area of lesbian aging for many years and has had a number of articles (many of them coauthored with Raphael) published in professional journals and books on this topic. A few places her work has been published: *Generations* (American Society on Aging), *Journal of Alternative Lifestyles* (SAGE), *The Sourcebook on Lesbian/Gay Health Care* (second edition, The National Lesbian and Gay Health Foundation), and *Women-Identified Women* (Mayfield Press, 1984). Robinson Meyer spends her time reading, working, and playing with Raphael and their dog, Jenny. She works hard on issues she cares about, trying to make the world a fairer place for lesbians and gay men.

THE MOVEMENT

We have had the unique opportunity to witness and observe the genesis of a new social movement. This movement, which is still giving birth to itself, is one we would broadly define as a movement to empower old lesbians. We wish to share some of our experiences and insights with the hope that the reader will learn that no one is too old to speak out for herself and her rights, transforming her world.

Until the late 1970s there was no body of literature on lesbian aging, no organization of old lesbians to contact, no completed research on this topic to cite. We who conducted research at that time found that old lesbians were invisible as a group, and often invisible to one another except through private social networks.

Old lesbians we knew both from movement activities and early research projects expressed interest in creating groups and environments that would better serve their own interests and needs. Many of these women participated in the heydays of the lesbian and gay movement (post-1969) and the feminist movement, but also reported their frustrations and anger at being the victims of ageist and often sexist behavior in those same groups.

The women who attended social and political groups at gay and feminist centers spoke of being tired of always being the oldest people—often the only ones over thirty—present. They said no one listened to them. Many had attended meetings for fifty years and knew how to get things done. Some thought the young women were often "reinventing the wheel"; they also felt they were putting their own concerns on the back burner because of the younger lesbians' differences in political styles and interests.

DEFINING AGEISM

Ageism has been defined in several ways. It can be viewed strictly as a form of discrimination against old people, or as discrimination against any given age group (most commonly the young or the old). Many writers have noted that women are most often the target of discrimination on the basis of age; author Susan Sontag called this the "double standard of aging."

In 1983 Barbara Macdonald with Cynthia Rich published *Look Me in the Eye: Old Women, Aging, and Ageism*, a book that received wide coverage and praise and that raised consciousness around issues of ageism for women and for lesbians. This was followed in 1985 by a lengthy Baba Copper article in the journal *Trivia*, "The View from over the Hill: Notes on Ageism between Lesbians," that specifically addressed issues of ageism for lesbians. The article "Over the Hill: Reflection on Ageism between Women," was later published as a book with additional contributions.

Many of the issues Macdonald and Copper raised in their respective writings set the tone for the April 1987 first West Coast Old Lesbian Conference and Celebration held at California State University, Dominguez Hills. Both of us attended and the group was addressed by Macdonald, Jeanne Adleman, and Shevy Healey. The three-day conference was preceded by a year and a half of struggle and planning. (Both authors served on the conference planning committee and Robinson Meyer became conference coordinator.)

Old women are often invisible in our society. Once past child-bearing age, they are traditionally viewed as not being very important or having much to contribute—unless they can serve younger people by babysitting and performing other household chores. They are also valued as the keepers of family history. Since many old lesbians either don't have children or don't choose to play out the traditional "grandmotherly" roles, they are left out of the equation. Professionals too often view old women/old lesbians as needing help, as people to be used as research subjects, or as providers of living history.

Old lesbians are seldom found working in mainstream lesbian and gay organizations; when they are, they complain of not being included in decision making of any importance. It is also interesting to note that contrary to the stereotype that has old or older lesbians always on the prowl to seduce young lesbians, it is young lesbians who search out old lesbians—often because they view old lesbians as the mothers they would like to have had or as the grandmothers who are there to serve them but seldom as equals.

FOCUS ON
SEXISM AND LESBOPHOBIA

Women have second-class status, lesbians even lower. If she is a lesbian of color and/or disabled and/or poor, as well as old, she has a triple or quadruple stigma. Gerontologists tend to assign traditional roles to old women. This is played out in senior centers and nursing home programs that generally do not apply to the strong, independent-minded old lesbian, which is what many of these women had to become to survive. An example: the focus on infants and children, who are brought into a nursing home to visit on the assumption that the presence of the very young will bring out the nurturer in the old woman as though that should be the most important aspect of her life.

Sexism is also seen in medical research, where men and conditions that primarily affect men are most often studied. Gay men are socialized as men. While some gay men have learned to recognize and discard their sexist behavior in their relationships with women, many have not. With rare exceptions the primary decision makers in the gay community are men.

Lesbians are not very visible to the larger society, consequently lesbian issues and agendas are seldom addressed. Part of the invisibility stems from the societal perception that lesbianism is primarily a sexual behavior. In practical terms this means that if you are not wearing a T-shirt proclaiming your sexual preference or walking down the street necking with your woman friend, you are likely to be assumed heterosexual. This only adds to the invisibility of old lesbians/women who are not seen as sexual because of age stereotyping (ageism) and because lesbianism is commonly viewed in sexual terms (lesbophobia).

It would be the rare exception to find a gerontological setting in which a lesbian could be open about her identity without major negative repercussions. This is true of lesbian workers of all ages as well as of old lesbians who are utilizing a particular program. There has been ostracism, embarrassment, the withholding of necessary services, even expulsion. While many gerontologists would proclaim their neutrality on this issue, few are willing to stand up and be counted as advocates for this very underserved group. The sad fact is that few service providers in the aging field have taken the time or trouble to educate themselves on this topic.

Mixed social groups comprising both old gay men and old lesbians are relatively rare. Although many gay centers offer meetings geared to those over fifty-five or sixty, it is primarily men who attend them. Many reasons can be given for lesbian nonparticipation in the groups; the overriding reason most women give, however, has to do with being made to feel like "the other." Either they are patronized or ignored, or they are made to feel they should be responsible for the thoughts and feelings of all old lesbians. There are also problems with the language gay men use. The old lesbians who attempt to integrate are expected to be good sports about sexist or lesbophobic remarks; if they attempt to correct it must be with good humor, not anger.

PLANNING THE CONFERENCE

A major issue of contention when the first West Coast Old Lesbian Conference and Celebration was planned was the policy that only lesbians over age sixty were welcome and could participate fully. This was a difficult dilemma for those of us on the committee who were under sixty but were committed to the endeavor's success. Several different scenarios played out simultaneously: since some of the old lesbians had lovers who were in their fifties it was decided that an old lesbian could bring her significant other to the conference as her guest, but women under sixty would be separately tracked; there were women of color under sixty who were welcome because racial parity was to be given high priority; the remaining younger women were on the committee because they had worked in the community in this area and/or had close friendships with old lesbians on the committee.

As this issue and others emerged, much dissension grew around the question of whether lesbians under sixty could vote on anything or only speak to issues. Those of us who were strong feminists and felt we had been disenfranchised by men or by heterosexual women when trying to work with them found ourselves feeling very frustrated.

On the one hand, we could understand a group wanting to empower themselves. Yet when had we, middle-aged lesbians who would soon be old lesbians ourselves, become "the other"—or worse yet, the enemy? It was a very painful time for all of us. Friendships of many years ended. Trust quickly eroded.

Two examples of friendship/organizational relationships ending follow. It is interesting to note that both cases involve couples rather than single individuals. Research has shown the strength and importance of lesbian couples, and no doubt there was at least some "mate-protection" going on in both instances.

The first example involved two couples. In each case one partner was considered an old lesbian and the other was in her fifties. The younger woman of one couple supported the "old lesbian" positions on the planning committee and in so doing fully supported her partner's positions. The other younger woman disagreed with some positions the old lesbians were taking and felt her opinions were not being valued; her older partner supported her, but also agreed with many of the larger group's positions. The breakdown in the friendship of the two couples happened not because of disagreement, but because of a perceived lack of trust and respect for the younger woman because of her age.

In the second example one couple consisted of younger lesbians (under sixty) and the other of one old lesbian and one under sixty. The younger couple began to feel it was not acceptable to speak out and disagree with the old lesbians on the committee, who appeared to be sending messages that they could be "seen but not heard." This went not only against the grain of independent-thinking lesbian activists, but also against behavior learned from the equality-minded feminist movement. Each couple felt they were being attacked by the other, although each would say *they* didn't attack anyone, *they* were standing up for the political principles in which *they* believed. In both cases close friendships/working relationships of some duration withered and died.

THE CONFERENCE

The conference and celebration took on a life of its own. Sometimes it seemed the less together the organizers were, the more together the conference itself was. Most of the women who attended were not aware of the problems among the organizers. There were other very important questions we had wrestled with and had come to agree upon that bothered some participants, and even kept some women away. The most significant of these, we believe, was the use of the word old. The conference organizers thought it very important to reclaim the word, thereby saying there is nothing *wrong* with being "old."

We should all stop using euphemisms. No more elders, or elderly, or seniors, or golden-agers. The term older is also not appropriate. What does it mean, after all? Older than what or whom? We on the committee received a lot of complaints from women who said, "I'm not coming to a conference for the *old*." And, "Why do you have to call yourself old? It's such an ugly word."

The answer is to empower. To name oneself. To reclaim. If we need any analogies, it has only been about two decades since the word "lesbian" was reclaimed, and women now call themselves proud lesbians. But until twenty years ago, it was a clinical term. Many before 1971 called themselves gay women, which in itself was self-naming, to get away from the more clinical "female homosexual." The term change from gay woman to lesbian came from a more feminist perspective—invoking a proud history recorded back to Sappho—that was independent of the gay men's movement.

More than two hundred women attended the conference, which by any measure was most successful. Old lesbians shared crafts, arts, held a dance, watched films, heard musicians, saw plays, listened to presentations, participated in conference sessions, networked, dialogued, made new friends and lovers, had reunions with old friends, and generally had their consciousness raised while at the same time making plans to combat ageism.

An example of the high caliber of the conference's work is the opening presentations, which addressed the questions What is ageism? How do old lesbians confront ageism in society, its institutions, in the women's movement, in young lesbians, in ourselves? How do we empower ourselves? How is the personal political?"

THE VISION

As far as we know, no other group of old people has ever challenged the ageist, sexist, and lesbophobic beliefs that are so ingrained throughout our society. This visionary group of women represents the leading edge of those who will no longer allow others to define who they are, where or how they should live, what they should do with their time or money, or how they should plan their futures.

In a sense, the old lesbians we are describing have put out a challenge to all. For those working in the field of aging they force a reexamination of the assumptions under which gerontologists work. They even dare to ask for whom the aging specialists are working. Us or themselves? For their own careers and paychecks or to help empower those they are supposed to be serving? For the rest of society, these old lesbians with their radical feminist ideas point out a new direction that could be the beginning of old people having more control over their lives and destinies. Think about a society where no one is ever considered "over the hill." Think about a society where an opinion is valued for its content rather than being prejudged by the speaker's age or gender. Think about a society where physical beauty is not equated with any one age group.

RE-LEARNING

We, who began our journey into studying lesbians from a gerontological perspective, were jolted out of a comfortable path that had been built on a number of myths. Those myths had to do with who we wished old lesbians to be rather than who they actually were and who they were becoming. We believed that by studying old lesbians we would learn something about what our old age would be in the future. We also thought we would be able to improve conditions for our own old age by knowing about and helping establish programs and organizations for the present generation of old lesbians. What we found instead were some individuals who were laying the groundwork for a new way of thinking about old age, women, and lesbians.

We learned that just as our ideas about what might be good for them in their old age were not true for them, what we ourselves think we might enjoy doing at seventy-five might not be true for us. Many of these women told us the thoughts they had in their fifties and early sixties about what they wanted to do with their lives in their seventies and eighties bore little or no resemblance to what they are now actually doing at these older ages. They said that as they have aged, their ideas about how they wished to live their lives have changed.

An important insight that came as a result of our involvement with the old lesbians arose after a serious reevaluation of our roles as both gerontologists and movement activists. We were used to considering ourselves "insider" sociologists who were able to eliminate the "we/they" dichotomy so commonly found in mainstream academic research. Finding ourselves on the "outside" of the group was a very uncomfortable experience that forced us to view old lesbians and their situations through their eyes rather than through our own.

We learned that while we felt solidarity with "their movement"—which will someday when we are old be "our movement"—in the present time frame we are not insiders. Some younger lesbians, including lesbian gerontologists, have felt rejected by what they perceived as a highly separatist and unyielding ideology; we, however, have to come to understand the necessity for old lesbians to take their own power and determine their own destiny.

TRANSFORMATION

We believe that what this small group of old lesbians has already achieved cannot help but affect a larger population. When we begin to change language, the very core of how we think about reality is transformed. When the word "old" is changed from a negative to a positive, or at least neutral, perception, it allows both user and listener to include the old as active and equal participants in whatever the endeavor is. It automatically empowers the individual. To reclaim the word "old" is to break down barriers that are there to keep people in their place, then to allow them to move along the path toward creating their own definition of what their later years might be. Thus the impact of this group of old lesbians goes beyond word usage and definition of old age: Words have become deeds.

In all respects, what propels this small but influential group of old lesbians who are redefining old age and fighting ageism is feminism, and a feminist understanding of women's reality. Although few women understand all the nuances of feminist theory, all women today are affected by the ideas of feminism. We believe that eventually the ideas brought forth by these pioneering old lesbians will find their way into the everyday lives of all people young and old.

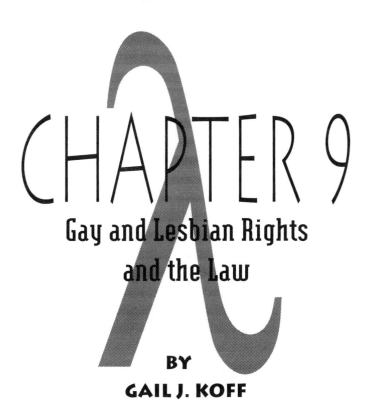

CHAPTER 9

Gay and Lesbian Rights and the Law

BY
GAIL J. KOFF

About the Author: Gail J. Koff, Esq., is a founding partner of the national Jacoby & Myers Law Offices. She oversees all East Coast operations from the firm's New York headquarters and is responsible for expansion and new business development. While in law school she worked in the Legal Services Corporation, an offshoot of President Johnson's War on Poverty program, and was later associated with the New York law firms of Gasperini & Savage and Skadden, Arps, Slate, Meagher & Flom.

Koff is the author of *The Jacoby & Myers Practical Guide to Everyday Law* (Simon & Schuster, 1986); *Love and the Law* (Simon & Schuster, 1989), and *The Jacoby & Myers*

Practical Guide to Personal Injury (Simon & Schuster, 1992). She has also written a series of legal guidebooks on such topics as personal bankruptcy, divorce, and mini-litigation for Henry Holt.

She and her husband, Ralph Brill, a venture capitalist and architect, have a modified commuter marriage. With their three children they share a house in New York's Hudson River Valley and an apartment in Manhattan.

λ

It has been only a decade or so since homosexual rights advocates have become openly vocal by lobbying in city, state and federal governments for gay rights legislation; running for and winning public office; holding gay pride marches in many major cities; and generally trying to make the public more aware of the serious problems resulting from the deep, ingrained prejudice they encounter each day.

Sometimes the bias is blatant, such as when homosexuals are fired from jobs or denied a place to live simply because of their sexual preference. Other times it is more veiled, such as when they are not hired for particular jobs though eminently well qualified or when they are ostracized socially. The social stigma of being gay or lesbian has and probably always will be with us; but now there is also the public's fear of AIDS.

Many of the problems homosexuals experience have been exposed in the past ten years, and as a result a growing number of people in the straight community have become somewhat more sensitive to the plight of gays and lesbians. Perhaps nowhere is this more evident, symbolically at least, than in the fact that finally, in 1987, the *New York Times* capitulated and began using the term "gay" in place of "homosexual" in news stories. (Incidentally, at the same time the newspaper also allowed the use of "Ms." in place of Mrs. or Miss.)

This growing public awareness has also had an impact on the law, which is undergoing an upheaval in an attempt to deal with the changes occurring in the social arena. Cases now reaching the court system promise to have a long-lasting effect on how gay men and lesbians are treated under the law. Further complicating the situation, however, is the fact that in many areas homosexuals are not only considered social pariahs but are also subject to archaic laws that have been on the books for a century or more that make their sexual practices illegal.

BREAKING UP IS HARD TO DO

Homosexual couples living together are susceptible to the same problems that can plague a heterosexual couple when they choose to end their relationship. Unfortunately, gay or lesbian couples are not always entitled to the same remedies. They cannot, for instance, protect their interests by getting married. And yet the situation is far from hopeless.

Take the case of Jim and Fred, who lived together for seven years. Jim was the wage-earner while Fred took care of the household duties. Together they accumulated property, including a Jaguar, a Lincoln Continental, and a house. The assets were registered in both names.

After a terrible argument that culminated in a violent fight in which Jim physically assaulted Fred, Jim threw Fred out of the house. With few assets of his own, Fred visited one of our offices in Southern California to see if he could get his fair share of the property he and Jim had acquired while living together.

Our attorney informed Fred that since both his and Jim's names appeared on the ownership papers of the property in question and since there was no marriage, nor could there be, they would ask the court for a partition agreement. (The concept of a partition comes to us from the days when this country's Western territories were being settled. Two ranchers might pool their resources and purchase property of, say, forty acres. Subsequently, if they couldn't get along and took their grievances to court, the courts would often move to partition the property, giving twenty acres to each rancher. This simple remedy has carried over to today.)

There is no way to split a house in half, so in Jim's and Fred's case the court may order the house sold and the proceeds apportioned accordingly. (Litigation usually results in a buy-out agreement.)

In many localities a case like this could take as long as five years to get to court. If possible, therefore, it may be wisest to work out some kind of equitable agreement. Taking his attorney's advice, Fred agreed to a negotiated settlement that gave him one of the cars, and Jim paid Fred a fair amount for his share of the house.

Even if property is in both parties' names, it might be a good idea to get some kind of written agreement. The reason is that having the house in both parties' names does nothing to help the person without funds with the expense of litigation if it becomes necessary. Many contracts between two people can include a clause concerning attorney's fees. This is helpful especially in a state like California, where the prevailing party in a lawsuit is not entitled to attorney's fees. In addition, it gives the nonworking party some leverage, making it easier for him or her to find an attorney willing to take the case.

Another possible alternative for a homosexual couple living together and sharing property is, in the case of a house, to take title as joint tenants with the right of survivorship, that is, if one party dies the property goes to the surviving partner.

TILL DEATH DO US PART

It is especially important for homosexual couples to have wills, primarily because the law will not treat them as a married couple.

The necessity for a valid will is apparent in the case of Howard and Terry. They had been living together for nearly five years when Terry found that he had AIDS. Realizing that he was dying, Terry had a will drawn up—leaving everything he owned to Howard. After months of lying ill, trying to fight off the several diseases that attacked his body, Terry did die.

Grieving over his lover's death, Howard was totally unprepared for what happened next. Terry's parents, who could never accept the fact that their son was gay, decided to contest the will, arguing that the disease he suffered from made him incompetent at the time he wrote it. Terry's parents had no interest in Terry's money or his property per se. They were motivated to take this action because they were extremely disturbed with their son's palpable admission—which took the form of his generous bequest to Howard—that he was a homosexual.

The case has not yet gone to court; but if and when it does, Terry's parents will have an extremely difficult time challenging the will, primarily because Terry's doctor can testify that his patient was competent at the time he wrote it. This case points out the necessity for a valid will. If Terry had died intestate—that is, without a will—all his possessions would have passed to his parents or, if he had no parents or close relations, to the state.

WILL HE OR WON'T HE?

Miguel Braschi and Leslie Blanchard met in 1976 and eventually moved into an apartment in Manhattan. The two men worked together in Blanchard's hair salon and shared bank accounts, income, expenses, and a credit card, and generally lived together as life partners until Blanchard died in the fall of 1986. In his will Blanchard left Braschi his entire estate, amounting to almost $5 million. The will was contested by Blanchard's family. This case, according to New York Supreme Court Justice Harold Baer, Jr., "demonstrates that a nontraditional unit [can] fulfill any definitional criteria of the term 'family.'"

There have been, of course, other cases regarding wills made by homosexuals that referred to particular and unique state laws. One such was the case of Danny Washington of New Orleans who was left property worth from $400,000 to $750,000 in the will of his lover, Samuel Wilds Bacot, Jr.; the will was written ten days before Bacot died in 1984. Louisiana has what is called a "concubinage" law that limits the bequests two people living together but only "pretending" to be married can leave each other. This limit would have allowed Washington to inherit only one-tenth of Bacot's "movable property," and none of his real estate.

The lower court's judgment was to turn over the bulk of Bacot's estate to a son he'd adopted two years before he died. The appellate court reversed that decision, however, ruling that the concubinage law did not apply to a homosexual relationship because the participants could not be said to be pretending to be married since marriage by two people of the same sex is illegal in Louisiana. In this case, then, Bacot's will was honored.

Undoubtedly the Braschi and Washington cases, like many others, will be appealed, and perhaps no definitive answers will be available until local and state legislatures are forced to deal with these matters. In the meantime, it's best to check the law in your state.

HOME IS WHERE THE HEART IS

Sometimes a problem arises in the case of a rental apartment when only one party's name is on the lease. What concerns us here is not who has rights to the apartment if the relationship breaks up, but rather what happens if the partner whose name is on the lease dies.

If a couple is married and the husband dies, his wife retains the right to the apartment. This is not necessarily the case with a homosexual couple, or for that matter with a heterosexual couple living together without any kind of agreement. There has been some litigation in this area recently, but the results have not been clear cut.

In 1987, for instance, a New York appeals court in Manhattan ruled that a homosexual whose lover died of AIDS had no right to the rent-stabilized apartment the two men shared because his name was not on the lease. In another case that same year, however, also in Manhattan, a judge ruled that a homosexual had as much right as a heterosexual to take over the lease of a deceased lover.

As one can readily see, this is yet another area of the law that is in flux, one in which legislation will probably be necessary to clarify the rights of those involved.

I OWE WHO?

When two people decide to live together, there is often the need to obtain credit, in the form of a car loan, credit card, or home mortgage, for example. Perhaps because one party is not working or has not established a line of credit, the burden may fall on the other party.

The most common example occurs when one person in the relationship has a credit card and the other doesn't. The one with the credit card may apply for an additional card for the other. Regardless of who actually uses the card, the individual whose name is on the account is responsible for the debts, and that is who the credit card company will go after. In fact, the only remedy the card owner has to collect the other person's fair share of the debt is to take that person to court.

This is often impractical, however—as in the case of Janet and Francine, a lesbian couple living together. Janet, an attorney, could easily attain credit, while Francine, in ill health, was unable to work. They enjoyed dining out at good restaurants and eventually managed to run up credit card debts, all in Janet's name, totaling close to $25,000.

After a time they ended their relationship. Francine had no money to pay her share of the debts. In any case, Janet was solely responsible for paying them because the cards were in her name. As a result she was forced to declare bankruptcy.

It's also wise to remember that when you co-sign a loan or acquire any kind of joint credit, the creditor will always go after the person with the most money, the one with the greatest ability to pay off the debt.

Another problem joint credit can create arose in the case of John and Frank. They lived together in a rental apartment for several years. Both had good jobs, and when their incomes increased to the point where it would put them in a better tax position, they decided to purchase a cooperative apartment. Each put up half the down payment and they split the maintenance equally. Then they decided to end the relationship.

Both were concerned about the payments due on the apartment. They knew if they failed to make them, the apartment would go into default and would be sold, probably at something below market value. As a result they approached one of our attorneys, and an agreement was worked out wherein John, who was making more money, would pay a higher share of the maintenance and, when the apartment was sold, would realize a greater proportion of the profits.

WHEN THERE'S A CHILD

In the past, the mere fact that one parent was an admitted homosexual meant he or she stood a good chance of being denied custody of a child. A parent's sexual orientation was often used to show that he or she would be an unsuitable role model for the child.

In many areas of the country this is still the rule rather than the exception. And yet today courts are beginning to ignore the sexual orientation of a parent and instead focus on the real issue: the ability to be a good parent.

In some states the courts, supported by expert testimony offered by psychologists, are rejecting the argument that a parent's sexual orientation should be the deciding factor in a custody battle. Instead they are using the criterion of "the best interests of the child," which might, under certain circumstances, be better served by the homosexual parent.

Yet homosexuals continue to be ruled out as custodial parents in many areas of the country, especially in those states that still have sodomy laws. In Virginia, for instance, where sodomy is outlawed, the state supreme court decided in the 1985 case of *Roe v. Roe* that a homosexual man was "an unfit and improper custodian as a matter of law."

What has helped liberalize the attitude of some courts in these cases is testimony by psychologists and other experts. One anonymous psychologist called as a witness in a Massachusetts case said, "There is no difference in the minor children and no evidence of sexual dysfunction to a minor child reared by a single homosexual parent." Furthermore, a 1985 survey concerning homosexual parents and their children, prepared by Dr. Robert J. Howell, professor of clinical psychology at Brigham Young University, found that "while custody decisions have tended to reflect stereotyped beliefs or fears concerning ... the detrimental effects of homosexual parenting practices on child development, a review of the research consistently fails to document any evidence substantiating those fears."

And, as reported in an article in the *New York Times* of January 1, 1987, Nan D. Hunter, director of the Lesbian and Gay Rights Project of the American Civil Liberties Union, said, "We are fighting very hard to establish the principle that a parent's behavior should not be considered by the court unless it has a negative impact on a child. It is a simple due-process principle, but it is amazing how difficult it has been to convince judges of it."

It's interesting to note that the courts in some states have become somewhat more liberal in this area. In New York State's Suffolk County, for instance, a judge recently granted custody of a child to a homosexual father.

THE GAY DIVORCÉE

While it is difficult for gay parents who live alone to be awarded custody of a child, it is almost impossible for a gay parent who resides with a live-in lover to win custody. Most courts have assumed that children will be disturbed living in a homosexual environment, even without clear evidence that this is so. Courts across the country have expressed grave concerns that children might be inclined or induced to follow a homosexual lifestyle if they are residing with a gay parent, with or without a lover present.

In a New York case, for example, the court ruled that although a lesbian mother was free to live any lifestyle she chose, she could not impose this lifestyle on her child. Other states, such as New Jersey and Washington, have granted initial custody to lesbian mothers but only on the condition that the mother not share the company of her lover when the children are present. New Jersey courts have gone so far as to award custody to a mother who was in an openly gay relationship.

Nevertheless, in determining custody most courts use homosexuality as but one factor among many. In other words, the mere fact of a parent's homosexuality is not supposed to automatically deny him or her custody of a child.

One interesting California case that was decided in 1987 involved a sixteen-year-old youth whose custody was awarded to his late father's homosexual lover. The court ruled that this was what the youth wanted, and it would give him the "stable and wholesome environment" his mother, who at one point had snatched the child, could not provide.

To sum up on the subject of homosexual custody, the standard for the courts remains what is in "the best interests of the child." And even though courts still appear to give the fact of homosexuality greater weight in determining its effects on those best interests, on the whole, few courts have held the mere fact of one parent's homosexuality in itself sufficient to deny that parent custody.

GAY ADOPTIONS

It was only a bit more than a half-dozen years ago that a California man became the first openly gay adoptive parent. This adoption cannot be said to have opened the floodgates for other gays who wish to adopt, but some have been successful in Alaska, California, and Oregon.

Other states have not been quick to pick up on this trend. In fact, several roadblocks have been set up to make it difficult, if not impossible, for gay or lesbian parents to adopt. Florida and New Hampshire laws ban adoptions by homosexuals (gay foster parents are also banned in New Hampshire); a Massachusetts policy prohibits the placement of foster children with homosexuals (this policy does not deal with adoptions); and Arizona, the only state with case law on the subject, has denied a bisexual man's petition to adopt.

WHO'S THAT
KNOCKING AT MY DOOR?

As difficult as it may be to believe, in some states homosexuality per se is against the law. The statutes involved, most of them on the books for over a hundred years, make sodomy a crime. In fact, such statutes raise the basic issue of the right to privacy. Though these laws are rarely if ever enforced, the mere fact that they may be used constitutes a Damoclean sword over the heads of homosexuals. Sometimes, as you will see in the following case, that sword actually does damage.

On August 3, 1982, an Atlanta police officer appeared at the home of Michael Hardwick to serve him with a warrant, issued because Hardwick had failed to pay a fine for public drunkenness. The man answering the door was asked by the officer if Mr. Hardwick was at home. He replied that he wasn't sure but the officer could check the house if he liked.

The officer then walked down a hall to a bedroom where the door was ajar. Inside he saw Michael Hardwick and another man performing oral sex. The officer immediately arrested both men and charged each with sodomy, a felony under Georgia law punishable by up to twenty years in prison.

Thus began a case that eventually made it all the way to the Supreme Court—and the controversial 1986 decision will undoubtedly have far-reaching effects on the right to privacy of homosexuals and heterosexuals alike.

Most Americans have always been under the impression that what we do in the privacy of our own homes is just that, private. But with this decision the Court chipped away at this concept by ruling that the constitutional right to privacy is not as all-encompassing as we might have thought or liked. Several authorities have even gone so far as to say that the decision in the Hardwick case was nothing less than a disaster for homosexual rights advocates.

Interestingly enough, the charges were never actually brought against Hardwick because the Fulton County district attorney refused to submit the charge to a grand jury unless there was further evidence. Nevertheless, Hardwick's attorney, Kathy Wilde, argued that this "left Michael in never-never land. The charge of sodomy could be reinstituted at any moment. That was the point at which he decided to challenge the law."

Michael Hardwick challenged his arrest for sodomy, which is defined by law as "any sex act involving the sex organs of one person and the mouth or anus of another," asserting that his rights of privacy, due process, freedom of association, and freedom of expression were abridged by his arrest.

A federal district judge initially dismissed the case on procedural grounds, but a three-judge panel for the United States Court of Appeals, taking up the case, ruled in May 1985 that the Georgia antisodomy law was unconstitutional. "The Constitution," the court held, "prevents the states from unduly interfering in certain individual decisions critical to personal autonomy because those decisions are essentially private and beyond the reach of a civilized society."

The case did not end there, however; the state of Georgia chose to appeal, arguing that sodomy is an unnatural act and a crime against the laws of God and man.

The state further argued that the law would help reduce the spread of AIDS.

The Supreme Court chose to hear the case and, on June 30, 1986, in a five-four decision, ruled that the Constitution does not protect homosexual relations between consenting adults even in the privacy of their own homes. Furthermore, the Court held that the Georgia law that forbade all people to engage in oral or anal sex could be used to prosecute such conduct between homosexuals.

In effect, the landmark ruling rejected what Associate Justice Byron White characterized as the view "that any kind of private sexual conduct between consenting adults is constitutionally insulated from state proscription." Justice White also noted that until 1961 all fifty states outlawed homosexual sodomy, and that twenty-four states and the District of Columbia still did.

Justice White further explained that the Hardwick case "does not require a judgment on whether laws against sodomy between consenting adults in general, or between homosexuals in particular, are wise or desirable. . . . The issue presented is whether the federal Constitution confers a fundamental right upon homosexuals to engage in sodomy and hence invalidates the laws of many states that still make such conduct illegal and have done so for a very long time." He, along with the majority of the Court, felt the Constitution does not.

WHERE WE STAND

Today twenty-six states have decriminalized sodomy, and five of the twenty-four that still make homosexual sodomy a crime have decriminalized it, at least in some contests.

Those states without sodomy laws are Alaska, California, Colorado, Connecticut, Delaware, Hawaii, Illinois, Indiana, Iowa, Maine, Massachusetts, Nebraska, New Hampshire,

New Jersey, New Mexico, New York, North Dakota, Ohio, Oregon, Pennsylvania, South Dakota, Vermont, Washington, West Virginia, Wisconsin, and Wyoming.

Those states that have heterosexual and homosexual sodomy laws are Alabama, Arizona, Florida, Georgia, Idaho, Kentucky, Louisiana, Maryland, Michigan, Minnesota, Mississippi, Missouri, North Carolina, Oklahoma, Rhode Island, South Carolina, Tennessee, Utah, and Virginia, as well as Washington, D.C. Those with homosexual sodomy laws only are Arkansas, Kansas, Montana, Nevada, and Texas.

As a result of this split in state laws, as well as of the 1986 Supreme Court decision, homosexuals appear to be far more vulnerable than heterosexuals concerning the regulation of their sexual practices. Thus a homosexual couple living together have an even thornier set of problems and possible pitfalls, as evidenced by the infringement of what some might consider one of the most basic of all rights, that of privacy.

Many cities and communities across the country are trying to balance the scales somewhat by passing homosexual rights laws. This is the case in New York City, where the city council, after rejecting a homosexual rights bill for fifteen years, finally enacted Local Law 2 on March 20, 1986. This law bans discrimination on the basis of sexual orientation in housing, employment, and public accommodations.

SEXUALLY TRANSMITTED DISEASES AND THE LAW

Fifteen years ago it would have been unthought of to have the law interacting with the social sphere in terms of diseases that can be sexually transmitted. But today, due in large part to the overwhelming concern caused by the spread of AIDS, the law is inextricably interweaved with these issues. People are reaching out to the law not only for protection but also for relief. One need only consider the following recent issues to see some of the changes the legal system is now forced to deal with:

▼ A Brooklyn woman sued her husband for giving her "AIDS phobia," claiming she was left paralyzed with fear after learning of her husband's homosexual activity. The case was thrown out of court because the judge ruled that if such suits were allowed, separate damage claims for "AIDS phobia" could be filed by any spouse who alleged adultery.

▼ A homeless New York man was charged with murdering a male friend who told him, immediately after they'd finished having sex, that he had the AIDS virus.

▼ A bill was introduced into the New York State legislature in 1988 that would permit doctors to warn sexual partners of AIDS patients that they may have been infected—even if the patients object to the disclosure.

▼ A Chicago woman filed a $12 million suit for damages against American Airlines after a scuffle in which she was allegedly bitten by a ticket agent who later tested positive for the AIDS virus. Although the woman tested negative for the disease, she sought compensation for "infliction of emotional damages."

▼ When a twenty-eight-year-old Los Angeles man infected with the AIDS virus left half his assets to a church run by his homosexual lover, his family moved to set aside the will, claiming that the lover had exposed the man to the virus.

▼ The rights of homosexual fathers to visit their children have been contested using the argument that the men are at high risk of contracting the AIDS virus and then passing it on to their children.

These are just a few examples of the many problems that have arisen over the past few years as a result of the rapid spread of various diseases that can be transmitted sexually, as well as in other ways. Without doubt the seriousness of the AIDS epidemic has propelled the courts and state legislatures into action.

Experts estimate that there are six hundred thousand new cases of AIDS reported each year. In addition, the number of cases of AIDS is expected to increase markedly over the next few years. As a result, increasing numbers of people who suffer from this disease are instituting lawsuits against those they believe knowingly exposed them to the virus. The lawsuits constitute attempts to obtain legal relief for both the physical and the emotional harm created by the diseases.

The precedents for these kinds of decisions, based on the theory of recovery due to negligence, began with an 1896 Wisconsin case in which the court held a householder liable for failing to warn a servant that a family member's typhoid fever was contagious. Twenty-four years later a Missouri court issued a similar decision concerning a smallpox case. In 1979 the Wyoming Supreme Court recognized the possibility of bringing a lawsuit against someone for negligently exposing another person to gonorrhea.

Battery has also been used to recover damages. The theory here is that the victim would not have allowed the person infected with the disease to touch him if he'd had informed consent, hence an unlawful battery was committed.

But no matter which theory is used, it must be proved that the transmitter knew he or she had the disease at the time of transmission. To maximize any recovery, it must also be proved that the plaintiff suffered both physically and emotionally.

Because of the nature of AIDS and other diseases, their gravity and the environment of fear they have created, it is likely that many more of these kinds of cases will find their way into the legal system. We consequently look for further legislation to be passed in this area.

Editor's note: Because laws are changing all the time and because they vary from state to state, we urge you to contact an attorney concerning current law where you live. To obtain the names of attorneys versed in homosexual rights, you may wish to contact some of the organizations mentioned in Chapter 10.

CHAPTER 10

Resources

BY
WILLIAM S. HUBBARD

About the Author: Will Hubbard is currently an adjunct instructor of gerontology at Virginia Polytechnic Institute and State University, where he is a Ph.D. candidate in adult development and aging. He holds a master's degree in gerontology from San Francisco State University. Hubbard grew up in Southampton, New York, and has lived in New York City and San Francisco. For the past three years he has lived in Blacksburg, Virginia, a rural university town in the foothills of the Appalachian Mountains. He is currently finishing a Ph.D. dissertation focused on the lives of gay men living in rural areas of the southern Appalachian region of the United States.

His spare time is devoted to activism and cultural work in gay communities. Hubbard can be contacted at 204 Washington St. SW, Blacksburg, VA 24060.

————————————————————| λ |————————————————————

Gay and lesbian gerontology is an emerging field of study that enjoys input from a variety of information sources. Among these are the arts and humanities, social, behavioral, and health sciences, and the lived experiences of aging, older, and old gay and lesbian persons. Knowledge concerning men's and women's journeys across gay and lesbian life courses has been marginalized within gerontology. This annotated resource chapter is intended as a tool of empowerment that educators, practitioners, and researchers can use in their personal and professional lives as they move gay and lesbian issues into the gerontological mainstream.

I introduce you to a variety of sources of information on issues of aging in gay and lesbian communities. I have attempted to offer an inclusive approach to these sources that emphasizes accessibility to a wide audience and can be considered suggestive rather than exhaustive.

ORGANIZATIONS

This section includes organizations that serve the needs of gay and lesbian persons of all ages and those that specifically target the needs of older gay men and lesbians. While services offered by some of these organizations are limited to specific geographic regions, the organizations' experiences may provide models for those working toward developing programs in their own geographic regions.

COMMUNITY DEVELOPMENT

Horizons Foundation is "a grantmaking community foundation dedicated to improving the human services for and the quality of life of lesbians and gay men" (Horizons *Foundation Newsletter*, 3(3), 1991). Horizons funds projects only in the San Francisco Bay Area and has funded a number of projects benefiting gay and lesbian elders. 870 Market St., Ste. 488, San Francisco, CA 94102.

EDUCATIONAL

Parents and Friends of Lesbians and Gays (PFLAG) helps parents and friends of gay men and lesbians understand gay and lesbian culture through education and social support. PFLAG actively advocates for the rights of gay and lesbian persons. PO Box 27605, Washington, DC 20038.

Short Mountain Sanctuary is a gay and lesbian-identified and -owned intentional community in rural and Appalachian Tennessee. It hosts educational and community development activities and provides a safe space within a heterosexist world for gay and lesbian people and their friends. The community also hosts gatherings every fall and spring that typically attract upwards of a hundred visitors who come together to share gay and lesbian culture and celebrate gay and lesbian life. Visitors are always welcome. PO Box 68, Liberty, TN 37095.

HEALTH

National Lesbian/Gay Health Foundation provides information and models of service delivery to the lesbian/gay communities and the American health-care system. The foundation offers an excellent publication, *Sourcebook on Lesbian/Gay Healthcare* (first [1984] and second [1988] editions). 1638 R St. NW, #2, Washington, DC 20009.

HISTORICAL

International Gay and Lesbian Archives maintains archives of lesbian and gay history and publishes a newsletter, *IGLA Bulletin*. IGLA, PO Box 38100, Hollywood, CA 90038.

Lesbian Herstory Archives maintains an archive of lesbian herstory. PO Box 1258, New York, NY 10016.

San Francisco Bay Area Gay and Lesbian Historical Society is an incorporated membership organization that seeks to preserve gay and lesbian history in the San Francisco Bay Area. PO Box 2107, San Francisco, CA 94126.

POLITICAL

National Gay and Lesbian Task Force is a national gay and lesbian rights organization with an activist agenda for social change. 1517 U St. NW, Washington, DC 20009.

Old/Older/Senior Lesbian/Gay Advocates is a political action group focused on increasing visibility of older gay men and lesbians in a variety of arenas. 1428 N McCadden Place, Los Angeles, CA 90028.

Old Lesbians of the Bay Area is a grass roots political action group focused on challenging ageism and heterosexism, and on expanding life options for old lesbians. 77 Waller St., San Francisco, CA 94102.

Old Lesbian Organizing Committee is a national steering committee of lesbians sixty and over who are committed to networking with old lesbians everywhere in order to confront ageism and heterosexism, develop and disseminate educational materials, facilitate the formation of new groups confronting ageism, and increase visibility for old lesbians within the national women's movement. PO Box 980422, Houston, TX 77098.

PROFESSIONAL

Committee on Lesbian and Gay Concerns of the American Psychology Association organizes presentations on gay and lesbian issues at the annual meeting of APA and publishes training and advocacy materials. 1200 17th St. NW, Washington, DC 20036.

Gay and Lesbian Accommodations for the Experienced in Years is a voluntary membership group interested in expanding housing options for older gay men and lesbians, particularly regarding the development of gay- and lesbian-identified long-term care and retirement communities. PO Box 170206, San Francisco, CA 94117.

Lesbian and Gay Informal Interest Group of the Gerontological Society of America provides networking opportunities for researchers working in gay and lesbian gerontology and brings gay and lesbian aging concerns into the center of vision at annual meetings of GSA. 1275 K St. NW, Ste. 350, Washington, DC 20005.

National Association for Lesbian and Gay Gerontology is a voluntary membership organization that promotes research, publications and service-delivery efforts focused on aging issues among gay and lesbian persons, and supports networking among professionals and older adults concerned with aging within lesbian and gay communities. Members have been instrumental in co-chairing the gay and lesbian gerontology tract at the annual meetings of the American Society on Aging. NALGG publishes a comprehensive annotated resource guide. 1853 Market St., San Francisco, CA 94103.

National Committee on Lesbian and Gay Issues of the National Association of Social Workers has been instrumental in developing printed educational and training resources. 7981 Eastern Ave., Silver Spring, MD 20910.

Task Force on Gay and Lesbian Issues of the Council on Social Work Education has been instrumental in bringing gay and lesbian issues into the social welfare curricula. 111 8th Ave., New York, NY 10011.

SOCIAL SERVICES

Gay and Lesbian Outreach to Elders (GLOE) provides direct services and an extensive variety of social programs to older gay men and lesbians, acts as advocate for older gays and lesbians, and provides educational resources on gay and lesbian issues of aging to the larger community. GLOE publishes a monthly newsletter. 1853 Market St., San Francisco, CA 94103.

Senior Action in Gay Environment (SAGE) is an intergenerational social service organization providing direct services to gay and lesbian older adults, and information, education, and resources on lesbian and gay aging issues. Annual memberships are available and benefits include a subscription to SAGE's monthly newsletter. 208 W 13th St., New York, NY 10011.

SOCIAL SUPPORT

Gay and Lesbian Elders Active in Minnesota (GLEAM) provides a friendly and safe environment in which older gays and lesbians can meet and socialize. Socials are held the second Sunday of each month. Contact GLEAM by calling the Gay and Lesbian Community Action Council. 310 E 38th St., Minneapolis, MN 55409.

Retired Seniors is a voluntary membership organization that provides mutual support and friendship to retired gay men and lesbians in northern Virginia. The group publishes a newsletter, *Galore*. PO Box 15720, Arlington, VA 22215.

G-40+ is a San Francisco social group open to gay men and lesbians age forty and older. Twice monthly meetings attract upwards of eighty attendees, mostly gay men. PO Box 6741, San Francisco, CA 94101.

HOTLINE

A team of trained counselors and advisers is available to discuss problems, refer clients to help in their area, or just listen.

National Gay and Lesbian Crisis Line. 800-SOS-GAYS. Weekdays 5:00 P.M. to 10:00 P.M. Sponsored by the Fund for Human Dignity.

SPECIAL NEEDS/INTEREST

A variety of topics of special interest to gay men and lesbians is offered in the included publications.

Alyson Publications (1990). *Alyson Almanac: A Treasury of Information for the Gay and Lesbian Community.* **Boston: Alsyon Publications.** *As its title suggests, this book offers a comprehensive guide to gay and lesbian community resources.*

Dotson, E.W. (1991). *Putting Out 1991: A Publishing Resource Guide for Lesbian and Gay Writers.* **San Francisco: Putting Out Books.** *Writers interested in publishing their work in publications of the gay and lesbian press will find this book especially helpful.*

Huber, J. T. (Ed.) (1992). *How to Find out Information About AIDS.* **New York: Harrington Park Press.** *Jeffrey Huber offers a comprehensive sourcebook that will be of interest to persons living with AIDS, helping professionals, and those involved in AIDS research.*

FOCUSING ON AGING ISSUES

Only a handful of books dealing specifically with gay and lesbian aging have been published during the past decade. This list offers a recent sampling.

Adelman, M. (Ed.) (1986). *Long Time Passing: Lives of Older Lesbians.* **Boston: Alyson Publications.** *Marcy Adelman has edited a collection of twenty-two personal narratives and four essay articles on aging-related issues.*

Berger, R.M. (1982). *Gay and Gray.* **Champagne-Urbana, Illinois: University of Illinois Press. Reissued by Alyson Publications in 1984.** *Using data collected through questionnaires and in-depth interviews, Raymond Berger offers an impressive account of aging-related issues among 112 older gay men.*

Copper, B. (1988). *Over the Hill: Reflections on Ageism Between Women.* **Freedom, California: Crossing Press.** *Baba Copper presents a feminist analysis of ageism.*

***Durable Dauntless Dykes* (1987). Selections from *The Writings of Durable Dauntless Dykes*. San Francisco: Gay and Lesbian Outreach to Elders.** *This is a collection of personal narratives and poetry written by and for older lesbians.*

Kehoe, M. (1989). *Lesbians Over 60 Speak for Themselves.* **New York: Harrington Park Press. Originally published as a special issue of the** *Journal of Homosexuality***, 16(3/4), 1988.** *Relying on questionnaire data from a nationwide sample of one hundred, Monika Kehoe discusses dimensions of aging among older lesbians.*

Lee, J.A. (Ed.) (1991). *Gay Midlife and Maturity.* New York: Harrington Park Press. Originally published as a special issue of the *Journal of Homosexuality*, 20 (3/4), 1990. *John Lee has edited a collection of thirteen research reports and essays. Margaret Cruikshank's chapter provides a concise and helpful review of the gay and lesbian gerontology literature. Collectively, these authors have made an important contribution to gay and lesbian gerontology.*

MacDonald, B. with Rich, C. (1983). *Look Me in the Eye.* San Francisco: Spinsters Ink. *Barbara MacDonald and Cynthia Rich provide a feminist analysis of aging-related issues.*

National Association for Lesbian and Gay Gerontology (1991). *Resource Guide: Lesbian and Gay Aging.* San Francisco: National Association for Lesbian and Gay Gerontology. *Updated regularly, this annotated sourcebook is a useful tool for locating information on gay and lesbian aging issues.*

Sang, B., Warshow, J., & Smith, A.J. (Eds.) (1991). *Lesbians at Midlife: The Creative Transition.* San Francisco, California: Spinsters Book Company. *This impressive collection of thirty-eight chapters includes essays, personal narratives, poetry, and research reports.*

Vacha, K. (Ed.) (1986). *Quiet Fire: Memoirs of Older Gay Men.* Trumansburg, New York: Crossing Press. *Seventeen personal narratives offer insight into aging among gay men.*

BOOK CHAPTERS

The listed chapters offer various treatments on subjects of interest to those concerned with gay and lesbian issues.

Adair, N. & Adair, C. (1978). "Elsa." In N. Adair & C. Adair, *Word Is Out* **(pp. 15-28). San Francisco: New Glide Publications.** *Nancy Adair and Casey Adair interview Elsa Gidlow, older lesbian poet.*

Adair, N. & Adair, C. (1978). "Harry and John." In N. Adair & C. Adair, *Word Is Out* **(pp. 231-248). San Francisco: New Glide Publications.** *The authors interview Harry Hay and John Burnside, elder statespersons of the gay liberation movement, and members of a long-term committed couple relationship.*

Allen, P.G. (1984). "Beloved Women: The Lesbian in American Indian Culture." In T. Darty & S. Potter (Eds.) *Women-Identified Women.* **Palo Alto, California: Mayfield Publishing.** *Paula Gunn Allen examines social roles available to lesbians of all ages in Native American societies.*

Berger, R.M. (1992). "Research on Older Gay Men: What We Know, What We Need to Know." In N.J. Woodman (Ed.) *Lesbian and Gay Lifestyles: A Guide for Counseling and Education.* **(pp. 217-234). New York: Irvington Publishers.** *Raymond Berger recommends future research agendas.*

Berger, R.M. (1990). "Older Gays and Lesbians." In R.J. Kus (Ed.) *Keys to Caring: Assisting Your Gay and Lesbian Clients* **(pp. 170-181). Boston: Alyson Publications.** *Grounded in his extensive research and clinical practice experiences among older gay men, Berger identifies and challenges commonly held myths of gay and lesbian aging and discusses practical implications of research findings.*

Berger, R.M. (1988). "The Nine Questions of Gay Male Aging." In M. Shernoff & W.A. Scott (Eds.) *The*

Sourcebook on Lesbian/Gay Healthcare (second edition) (pp. 73-77). Washington, D.C.: National Lesbian/Gay Health Foundation. *Berger explores the most common questions related to gay male aging.*

Berger, R.M. (1985). "Rewriting a Bad Script: Older Lesbians and Gays." In H. Hidalgo, T.L. Peterson & N.J. Woodman (Eds.) *Lesbian and Gay Issues: A Resource Manual for Social Workers* (pp. 53-59). Silver Spring, Maryland: National Association of Social Workers. *Berger looks at the myths behind gay and lesbian aging.*

Berube, A. (1989). "Marching to a Different Drummer: Lesbian and Gay GI's In World War II." In M. Duberman, M. Vicinus & G. Chauncey, Jr. (Eds.) *Hidden from History: Reclaiming the Gay and Lesbian Past* (pp. 383-394). New York: Meridian. *Allan Berube reports on his research among gay men and lesbians who served in the Armed Forces during World War II.*

Clunis, D.M. & Greene, G.D. (1988). "Growing Older Together." Chapter 16 of their book, *Lesbian Couples* (pp. 219-231). Seattle: Seal Press. *Merilee Clunis and Dorsey Greene use case histories to review issues facing lesbian couples as they age.*

Copper, B. (1990). "The View From Over the Hill: Notes on Ageism Between Lesbians." In J. Allen (Ed.) *Lesbian Philosophies and Cultures* (pp. 219-240). Albany, New York: State University of New York Press. Originally published in *Trivia: A Journal of Ideas*, (Summer), 1985. *From a feminist perspective, Copper offers a personal narrative that focuses on ageism in lesbian communities.*

Copper, B. (1988). "Mothers and Daughters of Invention." In H. Alpert (Ed.) *We Are Everywhere: Writings by and About Lesbian Parents* (pp. 306-322). Freedom, California: Crossing Press. *The author presents a personal narrative focusing on her parenting experiences.*

Copper, B. (1986). "Voices: On Becoming Old Women." In J. Alexander, D. Berrow, L. Domitrovich, M. Donnelly & C. McLean (Eds.) *Women and Aging: An Anthology by Women* (pp. 47-57). Corvallis, Oregon: Calyx Books. *The author offers a personal narrative that takes a critical perspective on traditional images of aging among women in the United States.*

D'Emilio, J. (1989). "Gay Politics and Community in San Francisco Since World War II." In M. Duberman, M. Vicinus & G. Chauncey, Jr. (Eds.) *Hidden from History: Reclaiming the Gay and Lesbian Past* (pp. 456-476). New York: Meridian. *John D'Emilio traces the emergence of distinctly gay and lesbian cultures in the United States.*

Dunker, B. (1987). "Aging Lesbians: Observations and Speculations." In Boston Lesbian Psychologies Collective (Ed.) *Lesbian Psychologies: Explorations and Challenges* (pp. 72-82). Urbana, Illinois: University of Illinois Press. *Grounded in her private practice as a psychotherapist and her own aging as a late-blooming lesbian, Buffy Dunker offers an essay on lesbian aging.*

Friend, R.A. (1990). "Older Lesbian and Gay People: Responding to Homophobia." In F.W. Bozett & M.B. Sussman (Eds.) *Homosexuality and Family Relations* (pp. 241-264). New York: Harrington Park

Press. Originally published in *Marriage and Family Review*, 14(3/4), 1989. *In the context of family relationships, Richard Friend presents a theoretical essay focusing on the development and practice of gay and lesbian identities.*

Gidlow, E. (1984). "Casting a Net: Excerpts from an Autobiography." In M. Cruikshank (Ed.) *New Lesbian Writing* (pp. 124-136). San Francisco: Grey Fox Press. *Elsa Gidlow writes a personal narrative from her life as an older lesbian.*

Goldberg, S. (1986). "GLOE: A Model Social Service Program for Older Lesbians." In M. Adelman (Ed.) *Longtime Passing: Lives of Older Lesbians* (pp. 236-246). Boston: Alyson Publications. *Sheryl Goldberg, a former co-director at GLOE (Gay and Lesbian Outreach to Elders), discusses the development and components of the GLOE program, offering suggestions to those interested in developing similar programming.*

Healey, S. (1986). "Growing to Be an Old Woman: Aging and Ageism." In J. Alexander, D. Berrow, L. Domitrovich, M. Donnelly & C McLean (Eds.) *Women and Aging: An Anthology by Women* (pp. 58-62). Corvallis, Oregon: Calyx Books. *From a feminist perspective, Shevy Healy discusses the hazards of ageism.*

Hooyman, N.R. & Lustbader, W. (1986). In chapter 2 of their book, *Taking Care: Supporting Older People and Their Families* (New York: Free Press), Hooyman and Lustbader include a section entitled "Lesbian and Gay Couples" (pp. 39-44). *Nancy Hooyman and Wendy Lustbader review caregiving challenges often faced by older gay men and lesbians and their families and offer intervention recommendations.*

Johnson, M.T. & Kelly, J.J. (1979). "Deviate Sex Behavior Imaging: Social Definition and the Lives of Older Gay People." In O.J. Kaplan (Ed.), *Psychopathology of Aging* (pp. 243-258). New York: Academic Press. *Myra Johnson and James Kelly offer a social constructionist critique of social roles typically made available to older gay and lesbian people.*

Kehoe, M. (1984). "The Making of a Deviant." In M. Cruikshank (Ed.) *New Lesbian Writings* (pp. 137-146). San Francisco: Grey Fox Press. *This is a personal narrative of Monika Kehoe's life as a lesbian.*

Kelly, J.J. (1980). "Homosexuality and Aging." In J. Marmor (Ed.) *Homosexuality: A Modern Reappraisal* (pp. 176-193). New York: Basic Books. *James Kelly reviews and challenges myths concerning gay and lesbian aging and offers intervention recommendations.*

Kimmel, D.C. (1979). Adjustments to Aging Among Gay Men. In B. Berzon & R. Leighton (Eds.) *Positively Gay* (pp. 146-158). Los Angeles: Mediamix Associates. *Douglas Kimmel offers a comprehensive review of gerontology research focused on gay men.*

Kimmel, D.C., Raphael, S.M., Catalano, D. & Robinson, M. (1984). Older Lesbians and Gay Men." In National Lesbian/Gay Health Foundation (Eds.) *Sourcebook on Lesbian/Gay Healthcare* (pp. 69-70). *Veteran researchers and practitioners Kimmel, Raphael, Catalano, and Robinson challenge myths of gay and lesbian aging with a concise review of research findings.*

Kirkpatrick, M. (1989). "Lesbians: A Different Middle Age?" In J.M. Oldham & R.S. Liebert (Eds.) *The Middle*

Years: New Psychoanalytic Perspectives (pp. 135-148). New Haven, Connecticut: Yale University Press. *Martha Kirkpatrick, in an expanded version of her 1989 article in* Women's Studies Quarterly, *compares challenges and benefits of lesbian middle age to those of nonlesbian middle age.*

Lee, J. (1978) "Aging Is a State of Mind." In K. Jay & A. Young (Eds.) *Lavender Culture* (pp. 424-429). New York: Jove/HBJ. *Julie Lee, a former representative of The Daughters of Billitis (the first national organization for lesbians), offers, through a personal narrative, a glimpse into her own experience of the aging process.*

Lee, J.A. (1987). "The Invisible Lives of Canada's Gray Gays." In V.W. Marshall (Ed.) *Aging in Canada: Social Perspectives* (second edition) (pp. 133-155). Markham, Ontario: Fitzhenry & Whiteside. *John Lee reports questionnaire and in-depth-interview data from a longitudinal study of the lives of fifty-four older gay men.*

Libert, R.S. (1989). "Middle-aged Homosexual Men: Issues in Treatment." In J.M. Oldham & R.S. Libert (Eds.) *The Middle Years: New Psychoanalytic Perspectives* (pp. 149-154). New Haven, Connecticut: Yale University Press. *Using case histories, Robert Libert discusses issues facing gay men at midlife. Readers expecting an overtly pro-gay essay will be disappointed.*

Lipman, A. (1984). "Homosexuals." In E.R. Palmore (Ed.) *Handbook on the Aged in the United States* (pp. 323-337). Westport, Connecticut: Greenwood Press. *Aaron Lipman offers an extensive and critical review of research on lesbian and gay aging.*

Martin, D. & Lyon, P. (1979). "The Older Lesbian." In B. Berzon (Ed.) *Positively Gay* (pp. 134-145). Los Angeles: Mediamix Associates. *Combining national survey data with their own experiences as older lesbians, co-founders of the Daughters of Billitis, community activists and educators Del Martin and Phyllis Lyon present an essay on lesbian aging.*

Moses, A.E. & Hawkins, R.O., Jr. (1982). "Aging." In A.E. Moses & R.O. Hawkins, Jr. (Eds.) *Counseling Lesbian Women and Gay Men: A Life Issues Approach* (pp. 190-197). St. Louis, Missouri: C.V. Mosby. *Grounded in a thorough review of literature and clinical practice experiences, Ellie Moses and Robert Hawkins offer a review essay with recommendations for social interventions.*

Poor, M. (1982). "Older Lesbians." In M. Cruikshank (Ed.) *Lesbian Studies: Present and Future* (pp. 165-173). Westbury, New York: Feminist Press. *Grounded in a review of literature and her experiences as a psychotherapist, Matile Poor writes an essay on lesbian aging.*

Raphael, S.M. & Meyer (Robinson), M.R. (1988). "The Old Lesbian: Some Observations Ten Years Later." In M. Shernoff & W.A. Scott (Eds.) *The Sourcebook on Lesbian/Gay Healthcare* (second edition) (pp. 68-72). Washington, D.C.: National Lesbian/Gay Health Foundation. *Building on their research and experiences as community activists and educators, Sharon Raphael and Mina Meyer discuss issues facing lesbians as they age.*

Raphael, S.M. & Meyer (Robinson), M.R. (1984). "The Older Lesbian: Love Relationships and Friendship Patterns." In T. Darty & S. Potter (Eds.) *Women-*

Identified Women. Palo Alto, California: Mayfield Press. Originally published in *Alternative Lifestyles*, 3(2), 1980. *The authors present research findings from in-depth interviews with twenty older lesbians.*

Riki (1975). "Aging." In K. Jay & A. Young (Eds.) *After You're Out* (pp. 215-217). New York: Pyramid. *Riki offers a personal narrative on aging as a lesbian.*

Shaffer, R.S. (1972). "Will You Still Need Me When I'm 64?" In K. Jay & A. Young (Eds.) *Out of the Closets: Voices of Gay Liberation* (pp. 278-279). New York: Jove/HBJ. *Ralph Shaffer presents a personal narrative on aging as a gay man.*

Swallow, J. (1986). "Both Feet in Life: Interviews with Barbara Macdonald and Cynthia Rich." In J. Alexander, D. Berrow, L. Domitrovich, M. Donnelly & C. McLean (Eds.) *Women and Aging: An Anthology by Women* (pp. 193-203). Corvallis, Oregon: Calyx Books. *Jean Swallow interviews lesbian activists/writers Barbara Macdonald and Cynthia Rich.*

Tobin, K. & Wicker, R. (1975). Phyllis Lyon and Del Martin. A chapter in their book, *The Gay Crusaders* (pp. 47-64). New York: Arno Press. *Kay Tobin and Randy Wicker offer a glimpse into the lives of lesbian activists Phyllis Lyon and Del Martin, co-founders of The Daughters of Billitis.*

Tully, C.A. (1992). "Research on Older Lesbian Women: What Is Known, What Is Not Known, and How to Learn More." In N.J. Woodman (Ed.) *Lesbian and Gay Lifestyles: A Guide for Counseling and Education* (pp. 235-264). New York: Irvington Publishers. *Carol Tully recommends future research on aging among lesbians.*

Vining, D. (1986). "Old Is Not a Four-Letter Word." In his book, *How Can You Come Out if You've Never Been In?: Essays on Gay Life and Relationships* (pp. 95-102). Trumansburg, New York: Crossing Press. *Donald Vining offers a personal narrative of his own journey across a gay life course.*

ESSAY AND REVIEW ARTICLES PUBLISHED IN PROFESSIONAL JOURNALS

This collection of articles explores a wide range of topics pertaining to the gay and lesbian experience.

Allen, P.G. (1991). "Who Is Your Mother? Red Roots of White Feminism." "Sinister Wisdom," 43/44(Summer), 224-234. Reprinted in a revised version in P.G. Allen's, *The Sacred Hoop—Recovering the Feminine in American Indian Traditions*. Boston: Beacon Press. *Paula Gunn Allen discusses the special importance of the social role of grandmother in Native American cultures. While this article does not specifically address lesbian issues, Paula Gunn Allen self-identifies as a lesbian in "Indian Summer," her chapter in Marcy Adelman's book* Long Time Passing: Lives of Older Lesbians.

Berger, R.M., & Kelly, J.J. (1986). "Working with Homosexuals of the Older Population." *Social Casework*, 67(4), 203-210. *Raymond Berger and James Kelly bring a wealth of research and clinical experience to an essay on the aging-related challenges faced by gay and lesbian elders and offer recommendations on improving service-delivery programs.*

Berger, R.M. (1982). "The Unseen Minority: Older Gays

and Lesbians." *Social Work*, 27(3), 236-242. *Berger reviews gay and lesbian aging research, challenges the helping professions to bring gay and lesbian aging concerns into the center of their practice vision; he also offers intervention recommendations.*

Catalano, D.M., Valentine, W.E., and Greever, L. (1981). "Social Services for Aging Gay Men." *Catalyst*, 12, 47-60. *Donald Catalano, William Valentine, and Lee Greever review gay aging research, discuss implications, and offer recommendations for service delivery.*

Cornett, C.W. & Hudson, R.A. (1987). "Middle Adulthood and the Theories of Erickson, Gould, and Vaillant: Where Does the Gay Man Fit?" *Journal of Gerontological Social Work*, 10(3/4), 61-73. *Carlton Cornett and Ross Hudson employ the theoretical perspectives of Erickson, Gould, and Vaillant to reveal research and practice implications for gay and lesbian gerontology.*

Dawson, K. (1982). "Serving the Older Gay Community." *Seicus Report*, 11(2), 5-6. *Ken Dawson, former executive director of SAGE (Senior Action in a Gay Environment), reviews challenges often faced by older lesbians and gay men as they access social services.*

Dulaney, D.D. & Kelly, J.J. (1982). "Improving Services to Gay and Lesbian Clients." *Social Work*, 27(2), 178-183. *Diana Dulaney and James Kelly find that social workers usually do not receive adequate training for effective practice with gay and lesbian clients of all ages. They include recommendations for improving the social work curricula.*

Friend, R.A. (1987). "The Individual and Social Psychology of Aging: Clinical Implications for

Lesbians and Gay Men." *Journal of Homosexuality*, 14(1/2), 307-331. *Through case histories, Richard Friend examines the intersection of social context and individual psychology as it impacts the meaning of age among gay and lesbian persons.*

Gwenwald, M. (1984). "The SAGE Model for Serving Older Lesbians and Gay Men." *Journal of Social Work and Human Sexuality*, 2(2/3), 53-61. Reprinted in R. Schoenberg, R.S. Goldberg, & D.A Shore (Eds.) *With Compassion Toward Some: Homosexuality and Social Work in America* (pp. 53-64). New York: Harrington Park Press, 1985. *Morgan Gwenwald discusses the development, organizational structure, programming, and goals of SAGE, one of two gay- and lesbian-identified social service programs targeting and serving the needs of older gay men and lesbians.*

Hodges, B. (1991). "An Interview with Joan and Deborah of the Lesbian Herstory Archives." *Sinister Wisdom*, 43/44 (Summer), 95-104. *Beth Hodges describes the herstorical development of the organization, Lesbian Herstory Archives, and identifies some of its present and future goals.*

Kehoe, M. (1986). "A Portrait of the Older Lesbian." *Journal of Homosexuality*, 12(3/4), 157-161. *Monika Kehoe offers a composite image of the older lesbian.*

Kehoe, M. (1991). "Caring for the Aging Homosexual." *Focus on Geriatric Care and Rehabilitation*, 4(9). *Kehoe discusses challenges faced by older gay men and lesbians in long-term-care settings.*

Kimmel, D.C. (1992). "The Families of Older Gay and Lesbian Families." *Generations*, 16(3), 37-38. *Grounded in his extensive experience as researcher, practitioner, and educator, and a review of literature, Douglas Kimmel places issues of lesbian and gay aging in the context of family relationships.*

Kimmel, D.C. (1978). "Adult Development and Aging: A Gay Perspective." *Journal of Social Issues*, **34(3), 113-130.** *Kimmel applies Levinson's developmental theory to his data from interviews with older gay men to move toward the formation of a gay standpoint developmental theory for gerontology.*

Kirkpatrick, M. (1989). "Middle Age and the Lesbian Experience." *Women's Studies Quarterly*, **1&2, 87-96.** *Martha Kirkpatrick compares challenges and benefits of lesbian middle age to those of nonlesbian middle age.*

Lee, J.A. (1987). "What Can Homosexual Aging Studies Contribute to Theories of Aging?" *Journal of Homosexuality*, **13(4), 43-71.** *John Lee offers an essay on the potential contributions of lesbian and gay aging research to sociological theories used in gerontology.*

Lipman, A. (1986). "Homosexual Relationships." *Generations*, **10(4), 51-54.** *Aaron Lipman provides a critical review of research on gay and lesbian aging issues with special attention to the context of intimate relationships.*

Macdonald, B. (1991). "Do You Remember Me? *Sinister Wisdom*, **43/44 (Summer), 85-89.** *From a feminist perspective, Barbara Macdonald writes a personal narrative focusing on ageism.*

Macdonald, B. (1990). "Politics of Aging: I'm Not Your Mother." *Ms*, **July/August, 56-58.** *From a feminist* *perspective, Barbara Macdonald examines the effects of ageism on women's lives.*

Noyes, L.E. (1982). "Gray and Gay." *Journal of Gerontological Nursing,* **8(11), 636-639.** *Linda Noyes's essay focuses on challenges older gay men and lesbians face in health-care settings.*

Patten, J. (1992). "Gay and Lesbian Families." *Family Therapy News***, October, 10, 34.** *In an essay written for family therapists, John Patten reviews challenges often encountered by gays and lesbians in their family relationships and offers intervention recommendations.*

Raphael, S.M. & Robinson (Meyer), M.K. (1982). "Focus on Lesbian and Gay Aging." *Association for Gerontology in Higher Education Newsletter***, 5(2).** *Relying on a review of literature, Sharon Raphael and Mina Robinson (Meyer) discuss issues facing older gay men and lesbians; they include an extensive reading and resource list.*

Raphael, S.M. & Robinson (Meyer), M.K. (1981). "Lesbians and Gay Men in Later Life." *Generations***, 5(1), 16-18.** *Raphael and Robinson (Meyer) offer a review of literature and discuss implications for research and practice among older gay men and lesbians.*

RESEARCH REPORTS IN PROFESSIONAL JOURNALS
Herein is a sampling of research findings appearing in various journals over the last two decades.

Berger, R.M. (1984). "Realities of Gay and Lesbian Aging." *Social Work***, 29(1), 57-62.** *Raymond Berger* *presents findings of an interview study of eighteen older gay men and lesbians and makes recommendations for the delivery of social services.*

Berger, R.M. (1980). "Psychological Adaptation of the Older Homosexual Male." *Journal of Homosexuality,* **5(3), 161-175.** *Using questionnaire responses from 112 older gay men, Berger offers findings on the psychological well-being and social relationships of older gay men.*

Deevey, S. (1990). "Older Lesbian Women: An Invisible Minority." *Journal of Gerontological Nursing,* **16(5), 35-39.** *Using mailed-out questionnaires, Sharon Deevey investigates health-seeking behaviors among seventy-eight older lesbians.*

Friend, R.A. (1980). "Gay Aging: Adjustment and the Older Gay Male." *Alternative Lifestyles,* **3(2), 231-248.** *Using questionnaire and in-depth interview data, Richard Friend presents findings on the relationship of coming out, support systems and gender role flexibility to late-life adjustment among older gay men.*

Gray, H., & Dressel, P. (1985). "Alternative Interpretations of Aging Among Gay Males." *Gerontologist,* **25(1), 83-87.** *Heather Gray and Paula Dressel, using data from Karla Jay's and Allen Young's national data on life issues of gay men and lesbians (*The Gay Report. *New York: Summit Books, 1979), posit and test four hypotheses related to gay male aging.*

Kehoe, M. (1986). "Lesbians Over 65: A Triply Invisible Minority." *Journal of Homosexuality,* **12, 139-152.** *Kehoe uses questionnaire data from a national sample to explore the lived experiences of older lesbians.*

Kelly, J.J. (1977). "The Aging Male Homosexual: Myth and Reality." *The Gerontologist*, 17(4), 328-332. Reprinted in M. Levine (Ed.) *Sociology of Male Homosexuality* (253-262). New York: Basic Books. *James Kelly gathered data using questionnaires, interviews and participant observations to explore the older gay man's journey across the life course.*

Kimmel, D.C. (1979-1980). "Life-History Interviews of Aging Gay Men." *International Journal of Aging and Human Development*, 10(3), 239-248. *Kimmel presents findings from in-depth interviews with fourteen older gay men and discusses research and practice implications.*

Kimmel, D.C. (1977). "Psychotherapy and the Older Gay Man." *Psychotherapy: Theory, Research, and Practice*, 14(4), 386-393. *Findings from an exploratory study of aging among older gay men drive a discussion of challenges and opportunities unique to gay men as they age and related implications for psychotherapeutic practice.*

Lee, J.A. (1989). "Invisible Men: Canada's Aging Homosexuals. Can They Be Assimilated into Canada's Liberated Gay Communities?" *Canadian Journal on Aging*, 8(1), 79-97. *With data from two studies, John Lee reports challenges older gay men face as they access liberated gay communities.*

Lucco, A.J. (1987). "Planned Retirement Housing Preferences of Older Homosexuals." *Journal of Homosexuality*, 14(3/4), 55-36. *Using mail-out questionnaires, Lucco collected data from 456 lesbians and gay men to examine preferences for retirement housing options.*

Minnigerode, F.A. & Adelman, M.R. (1978). "Elderly Homosexual Women and Men: Report on a Pilot Study." *The Family Coordinator*, 27(4), 451-456. *Fred Minnigerode and Marcy Adelman present their research findings from in-depth interviews with eleven older gay men and lesbians.*

Nestle, J. (1991). Surviving and More: Interview with Mabel Hampton." *Sinister Wisdom*, 43/44 (Summer), 90-94. *Joan Nestle offers a glimpse into the life of Mabel Hampton, a seventy-seven-year-old African-American lesbian, and includes a picture of Hampton.*

Quam, J.K. & Whitford, G. (1992). "Adaptation and Age-Related Expectations of Older Gay and Lesbian Adults." *Gerontologist*, 32(3), 367-374. *Responding to questionnaires, eighty age fifty and older gay men and lesbians in Minnesota were asked to share information on their social relationships and satisfaction with life.*

Raphael, S.M. & Robinson, M.K. (1980). "The Older Lesbian: Love Relationships and Friendship Patterns." *Alternative Lifestyles*, 3(2), 207-209. *Sharon Raphael and Mina Robinson (Meyer) present research findings from in-depth interviews with twenty older lesbians. The authors' design and use of qualitative methods and attention to detail in analysis and interpretation are exemplary.*

Tully, C. T. (1989). "Caregiving: What Do Midlife Lesbians View as Important?" *Journal of Gay and Lesbian Psychotherapy*, 1(1), 87-103. *Using data collected from seventy-three midlife lesbians, Carol Tully describes caregiving needs midlife lesbians view as important, and their ability to meet these needs in their own communities as they age.*

ESSAYS IN GAY AND NONGAY POPULAR PRESS

The listed essays explore the gay and lesbian experience in a multitude of literary ways.

Alpenglow, R. (1986). "Changing Lives: A New GLOE for San Francisco." *The Bridge*, 2(3). *Robin Alpenglow describes the GLOE program.*

Angle, P. (1983). "Gay Seniors: Double Discrimination." *Tenderloin Times*, August, 4-5. *Pat Angle discusses the Gay and Lesbian Outreach to Elders Program's work among inner-city gay and lesbian elders in San Francisco.*

Bauer, A. (1992). "First U.S. Gay and Lesbian Conference on Aging Hits Homophobia/Ageism. *Aging Today*, 13(4), 1-2. *Amanda Bauer reports on the first national conference on gay and lesbian aging.*

Bennett, J. (1992). "As the Old Men Wait, the Talk Is of AIDS." *New York Times*, September 21, 41. *Through the voices of members of a support group for HIV-positive older gay men, James Bennett discusses AIDS-related challenges often facing older gay men.*

Berzon, B. (1992). "Why Are Older Gays and Lesbians Treated Like Pariahs?" *Advocate*, January 28, 1992, 98. *Based on her many years of clinical practice as a psychotherapist and her personal experiences of aging as a lesbian, Betty Berzon discusses ageism directed at and experienced by gay and lesbian persons.*

Cockrell, C. (1988). "The Graying of the Gay Community." *San Francisco Sentinel*, 16(21), 1,8-9,13. *Cathy Cockrell discusses issues facing older gay men and lesbians and discusses the GLOE model of social intervention. Photographs of GLOE participants and administrators are included.*

Connolly, L. (1992). "History Through the Eyes of Our Elders." *The Latest Issue* **(A Sacramento, California, news magazine for the gay community and its friends), 4(5), 1,16.** *Laura Connolly discusses issues of pre- and postliberation gay and lesbian culture through the eyes of gay and lesbian elders in Sacramento. Included are photographs of gay and lesbian elders, some of whom are well-known figures of the gay and lesbian liberation movement.*

GLOE Senior Writers Workshop (1986). "Selections From the GLOE Senior Writers Workshop." *Workshop Words,* **7 (Spring).** *This is a collection of prose and poetry from gay and lesbian older adults in San Francisco.*

Hubbard, W.S. (1991). "Lesbian and Gay Aging: Deconstructing Closets in Rural America." *RFD,* **68, 50-54. Reprinted in** *Country Faggot,* **2, 5-8. [***Country Faggot*** (CF) is a newsletter written by and for rural gay men and lesbians in Northern California.] PO Box 76, Honeydew, CA.** *Grounded in a review of gay and lesbian aging research and personal research among rural gay men, William Hubbard discusses issues among rural populations of older gay and lesbian persons.*

Hubbard, W.S. (1991). "Lesbian and Gay Aging: Exploring Myths." *Blue Ridge Lambda Press,* **November/December, 3. [***The Blue Ridge Lambda Press*** is the newsletter of the Roanoke Valley Gay and Lesbian Alliance (RVGLA), a socio-political group addressing the needs of urban and rural gay men and lesbians in central**

and southwest Virginia. RVGLA, PO Box 237, Roanoke, VA 24002.] *With a rural focus, this articles by Hubbard introduces and challenges some commonly held myths of gay and lesbian aging.*

Hubbard, W.S. (1991). "Invisible Minorities: Lesbian and Gay Elders." *The New River Free Press*, September/October, 7. [The New River Free Press is an alternative newspaper from southwest Virginia: PO Box 846, Blacksburg, VA 24063.] *With a rural focus, this articles by Hubbard introduces and challenges some commonly held myths of gay and lesbian aging.*

Kimmel, D.C. (1977). "Patterns of Aging Among Gay Men." *Christopher Street*, 2 (5/November). *Grounded in his research and clinical practice experiences, Douglas Kimmel discusses aging among gay men.*

Longcope, K. (1991). "Gay and Gray." *Boston Globe*, April 23, 57,61. *Kay Longcope offers a gay and lesbian perspective on aging issues through interviews with Boston-area gay and lesbian older adults.*

Mays, V. (1991). Older Gays and Lesbians: Their Dreams and Challenges." *Senior Spectrum*, 10(7), 1, 18, 31. *Through interviews with researchers and local gay and lesbian elders, Verna Mays discusses challenges and rewards associated with aging as a gay man or lesbian.*

Short Mountain Sanctuary (Eds.) (1984). "Agelessness Issue," a special Issue of *RFD*, 42 (Spring). [*RFD* is a quarterly journal self-described as a country journal for gay men everywhere. It is available by subscription and published by Short Mountain Sanctuary, PO Box 68, Liberty, TN 37095.] *The issue includes essays on ageism.*

BOOKS ON GAY AND LESBIAN CULTURE WITH RELEVANCE TO LESBIAN AND GAY AGING

Individual gay and lesbian lives, taken collectively, offer insight into the development of gay and lesbian culture and community as we understand it today. With this in mind, I include resources that focus on the emergence of contemporary gay and lesbian communities and cultures in the United States.

Adair, N. & Adair, C. (1978). *Word Is Out.* **San Francisco: New Glide Publications.** *A landmark book in gay and lesbian studies uses interview transcripts to examine the effects of gay and lesbian liberation on individual lives and community building.*

Berube, A. (1990). *Coming Out Under Fire: The History of Gay Men and Women in World War II.* **New York: Plume.** *Many of today's older gay men and lesbians share the experience of having served in the Armed Forces during World War II. Allan Berube examines the importance of sociopolitical changes generated by the war on the development of gay and lesbian culture. Includes photographs.*

Cruikshank, M. (1992). *The Gay and Lesbian Liberation Movement.* **New York: Routledge.** *Margaret Cruikshank has done a great service to the gay and lesbian communities. Taking a feminist perspective, she has written a very accessible and scholarly account of the development of gay and lesbian liberation and the development of contemporary gay and lesbian culture.*

Curtis, W. (Ed.) (1988). *Revelations: A Collection of Gay Male Coming Out Stories.* **Boston: Alsyon.** *Many believe that coming out represents the most important turning* *point in the lives of gay men and lesbians. Wayne Curtis's collection includes stories of gay men who have come out in late life.*

Duberman, M. (1991). *Cures: A Gay Man's Odyssey.* **New York: Plume.** *Martin Duberman offers an autobiographical account of coming to terms with a gay identity.*

D'Emilio, J. (1986). *Sexual Politics, Sexual Communities: The Making of a Homosexual Minority in the United States 1940-1970.* **Chicago: University of Chicago Press.** *John D'Emilio, a historian, offers a scholarly and accessible account of the development of contemporary gay and lesbian communities in the United States.*

Duberman, M., Vicinus, M. & Chauncey, G., Jr. (Eds.) (1989) *Hidden from History: Reclaiming the Gay and Lesbian Past.* **New York: Meridian.** *An impressive collection of essays focuses on bringing visibility to gay and lesbian contributions to history.*

Hall Carpenter Archives/Gay Men's Oral History Group (Eds.) (1989). *Walking After Midnight: Gay Men's Life Stories.* **London: Routledge.** *This volume includes the experiences of older gay men in the United Kingdom.*

Herdt, G. (Ed.) (1992) *Gay Culture in America: Essays from the Field.* **Boston: Beacon.** *An impressive edited collection of research-based essays, Gilbert Herdt's book provides us with new information and concise analyses of contemporary gay male culture.*

Gonsoriek, J.C. & Weinrich, J.D. (Eds.) (1991).

Homosexuality: Research Implications for Public Policy. **Newbury Park, California: SAGE.** *This volume provides information and recommendations for understanding and negotiating the critical link between research and political action.*

Jay, K. & Young, A. (Eds.) (1972). *Out of the Closets: Voices of Gay Liberation.* **New York: Jove/HBJ.** *Karla Jay and Allen Young are pioneers in gay and lesbian studies. This book will be of special interest to those who were active in gay and lesbian liberation during the decade of the 1970s and those who want to know more about that period in gay and lesbian history.*

Jay, K. & Young, A. (Eds.) (1978). *After You're Out.* **New York: Pyramid.** *Likewise, this book will be of special interest to those who were active in gay and lesbian liberation during the decade of the 1970s or are interested in this period.*

Jay, K. & Young, A. (Eds.) (1978). *Lavender Culture.* **New York: Jove/HBJ.** *More on gay and lesbian liberation during the decade of the 1970s.*

Kleinberg, S. (1980) *Alienated Affections.* **New York: St. Martin's Press.** *In a chapter entitled "Those Dying Generations: Harry and His Friends," Seymour Kleinberg describes social and psychological dimensions of the lives of four older gay men.*

Martin, D. & Lyon, P. (1972). *Lesbian/Woman.* **New York: Bantam Books.** *Del Martin and Phyllis Lyon, pioneering activists for lesbian and gay rights, provide one of the early accounts of the development and dimensions of lesbian culture in the United States.*

BOOK REVIEWS

These reviews look at significant books that have appeared dealing with the issues of gay and lesbian aging.

Almvig, C. (1982). A review of R.M. Berger's *Gay and Gray*. *Seicus Report*, November, 18.

Calasanti, T.M. (1992). "Theorizing About Gender and Aging: Beginning with the Voices of Women." *Gerontologist*, 32(2), 280-281.

Lee, J.A. (1987). A review of M. Adelman (Ed.), *Long Time Passing: Lives of Older Lesbians. Canadian Journal on Aging*, 6(3), 250-255.

Steinman, R. (1983). A review of R.M. Berger's *Gay and Gray. Journal of The American Geriatric Society*, 31(10), 629-630.

Randall, M. (1986). A review of B. Copper *Look Me in the Eye: Old Women, Aging and Ageism*. In J. Alexander, D. Berrow, L. Domitrovich, M. Donnelly & C. McLean (Eds.) *Women and Aging: An Anthology by Women*. Corvallis, Oregon: Calyx Books, 222-223.

Weg, R.B. (1987). A review of K. Vacha (Ed.) (1986). *Quiet Fire: Memoirs of Older Gay Men*. Trumansburg, New York: Crossing Press. *Gerontologist*, 27(1), 122-123.

DOCTORAL DISSERTATIONS

The included dissertations show the importance of having an academic forum for the exploration of gay and lesbian aging issues.

Adelman, M. (1980). *Adjustment to Aging and Styles of Being Gay: A Study of Elderly Gay Men and Lesbians*. Unpublished doctoral dissertation, The Wright Institute, Berkeley, California. *Marcy Adelman investigates psychosocial adjustment to aging among older gay men and lesbians.*

Goodwin, J.P. (1984). *More Man Than You'll Ever Be: Gay Folklore and Acculturation*. Unpublished Ph.D. dissertation, Indiana University, Bloomington. *Relying on participant observation and in-depth interviews, Joseph Goodwin investigates ways in which gay men learn about, access and invest in gay culture. This study, while not specifically focused on aging-related issues, is a classic piece of research on gay culture.*

Kelly, J.J. (1974). *Brothers and Brothers: The Gay Man's Adaptation to Aging*. Unpublished Ph.D. dissertation, Brandeis University, Waltham, Massachusetts. *Using questionnaires, in-depth interviews and participant observation, James Kelly investigates dimensions of aging among 240 self-identified gay men.*

Tully, C.T. (1980). *Social Support Systems of a Selected Sample of Older Women*. Unpublished doctoral dissertation, Virginia Commonwealth University, Richmond. *Carol Tully investigates social support networks among older lesbians.*

MASTER'S THESES
Lesbian invisibility is the core subject in these theses.

Almvig, C. (1982) *The Invisible Minority: Aging and Lesbianism*. Syracuse: Utica College of Syracuse. *Chris*

Almvig uses questionnaires to gather descriptive information on twenty-five lesbians over age sixty. Almvig is a co-founder of SAGE.

Devey, S. (1988). *Health-Seeking Behaviors in an Invisible Minority: Lesbian Women Over 50*. Unpublished master's thesis. Ohio State University, Columbus. *Sharon Deevey reports on her research among seventy-eight older lesbians that focuses on health-seeking behaviors.*

Robinson, (Meyer) M.K. (1979). *The Older Lesbian*. Unpublished master's thesis. California State University, Dominguez Hills, Carson. *A classic piece of qualitative research and the first systematic research conducted among older lesbians, Mina Robinson (Meyer) conducts multiple in-depth interviews among twenty older lesbians.*

CONFERENCE PAPERS

The listed papers provide a significant transfer of information regarding the diversity of the older gay and lesbian community.

Adams, C.L. & Kimmel, D.C. (1991, November). "Older African-American Gay Men." Paper presented at the 44th annual meeting of the Gerontological Society of America, San Francisco. Contact Douglas Kimmel, Ph.D., City College/CUNY, Department of Psychology, NY 10031. *Clarence Adams and Douglas Kimmel offer findings from in-depth interviews with twenty older African-American gay men. These researchers are the first to investigate issues of aging among this group.*

Boxer, A.M. (1992, November). "Middle-Aged Parents' Acceptance of Their Gay Male/Lesbian Adult Children."

Paper presented at the 45th annual meeting of the Gerontological Society of America, Washington, D.C. Contact Andrew Boxer, Ph.D., The Evelyn Hooker Center for Gay and Lesbian Mental Health, Department of Psychiatry, University of Chicago, 5327 N. Sheridan Rd., Chicago, IL 60640. *Using data from interviews with fifty parents of adult gay and lesbian persons, Andrew Boxer discusses issues facing parents as they learn of their children's investments in gay and lesbian identities.*

Hubbard, W.S. (1992, November) "Speaking of Invisibility: Finding the Life Histories of Aging Rural Gay Men." Paper presented at the 45th annual meeting of the Gerontological Society of America, Washington, D.C. Contact Will Hubbard, 204 Washington St. SW, Blacksburg, VA 24060. *Using data from ten in-depth interviews, William Hubbard offers information on the lives of gay men living in rural areas of the southern Appalachian region.*

Hubbard, W.S. & Allen, K.R. (1991, November). "Caregiving Contexts Among Older Gay Male Couples in a Rural Environment." Paper presented at the 44th annual meeting of the Gerontological Society of America, San Francisco. Address correspondence to Will Hubbard. *Using data from in-depth interviews, Hubbard and Katherine Allen discuss the caregiving careers of six older gay men living in the rural Southeast.*

Hubbard, W.S., Duke, M., Durham, P., Palmisano-Morales, R. &Roosen, G. (1992, March). "Gay and Lesbian Outreach to Elders (GLOE): San Francisco's Answer to Social Services for Older Lesbians and Gay Men." Paper presented at the 38th annual meeting of the American Society on Aging, San Diego. Address correspondence to Will Hubbard. *With data from thirty-eight in-depth interviews with GLOE participants, volunteers and administrators, the authors discuss the evolution of the GLOE model of service delivery.*

Kochman, A. & Anderson, G. (1991, November). "The Invisible Minority: Service Delivery to Gay and Lesbian Seniors." Paper presented at the 44th annual meeting of the Gerontological Society of America, San Francisco. Contact Arlene Kochman and Gregory Anderson, SAGE, 208 W 13th St., New York, NY 10011. *Arlene Kochman and Gregory Anderson discuss issues facing older gay male and lesbian participants in the SAGE program, and offer recommendations for social intervention.*

Kuckolek, K.J. (1992, March). "Attitudes of Gays and Lesbians Toward Service Preferences in Retirement Communities." Paper presented at the 38th annual meeting of the American Society on Aging, San Diego. Contact Kevin Kuckolek, Department of Sociology, Cleveland State University, Cleveland, Ohio. *Kevin Kuckolek presents findings from original research among 102 gay men and lesbians at all stages of adulthood concerning their preferences for institutionally based housing services.*

MacLeod, B. (1989, March). "Gay Men and Lesbians: Issues in Aging." Paper presented at the 35th annual meeting of the American Society on Aging, Washington, D.C. Contact Beth MacLeod, National Association for Gay and Lesbian Gerontology, 1853 Market St., San Francisco, CA 94103. *Beth MacLeod reviews challenges faced by older gay men and lesbians and those who design and implement social and health programs targeting their needs.*

Raphael, S.M. & Meyer, M.K. (1991, November). "Old Lesbians Deconstructing Ageism: Signposts to the Future." Paper presented at the 44th annual meeting of the Gerontological Society of America, San Francisco. Contact Sharon Raphael and Mina Meyer, California State University, Dominguez Hills, Department of Sociology, 100 E Victoria, Carson, CA 90747. *Sharon Raphael and Mina Meyer discuss heterosexist assumptions operating in gerontology and older-lesbian challenges to these assumptions.*

Zimmerman, S. (1991, November) "Identity and History: The Elder Lesbian." Paper presented at the 44th annual meeting of the Gerontological Society of America, San Francisco. Contact Sandra Zimmerman, University of San Francisco, Department of Family Health Care Nursing, San Francisco, CA 94143. *Using data from multiple in-depth life history interviews with twelve older lesbians, Sandra Zimmerman discusses issues facing older lesbians.*

EDUCATIONAL AND TRAINING RESOURCES

Educators will find these resources helpful as they develop and implement courses and training programs regarding gay and lesbian life issues.

ESSAYS AND REPORTS

Brown, L.S. (1989). "Lesbians, Gay Men and Their Families: Common Clinical Issues." *Journal of Gay and Lesbian Psychotherapy*, 1(1), 65-77. *Laura Brown reviews challenges gay men and lesbians often face in their family relationships and offers educational and practical intervention recommendations.*

Brown, L.S. (1989). "New Visions, New Voices: Toward a Lesbian/Gay Paradigm for Psychology." *Psychology of Women Quarterly*, 13, 445-458. *Brown outlines the emergence of a gay and lesbian standpoint theoretical perspective. This article will be of interest to researchers and others who have been searching for a clear articulation of a theoretical perspective that is grounded in gay and lesbian realities.*

Committee on Gay and Lesbian Concerns (1991). "Avoiding Heterosexual Bias in Language." *American Psychologist*, 46(9), 973-974. *The authors suggest the use of terminologies that can help eliminate heterosexism in contemporary language.*

Crumpacker, L. & Vander Haegen, E.M. (1987). "Pedagogy and Prejudice: Strategies for Confronting Homophobia in the Classroom." *Women's Studies Quarterly*, 15(3/4), 65-73. *Employing a feminist theoretical perspective, Laura Crumpacker and Eleanor Vander Haegen offer classroom strategies and exercises designed to diminish homophobia among college and university students.*

Herek, G.M., Kimmel, D.C., Amaro, H. & Melton, G.B. (1991). "Avoiding Heterosexist Bias in Psychological Research." *American Psychologist*, 46(9), 957-963. *Gregory Herek, Douglas Kimmel, Hortensia Amaro, and Gary Melton describe the ways in which heterosexist bias can occur in research and suggest ways to avoid it.*

Hubbard, W.S. (1991, February). "Focusing on an Invisible Minority: Integrating Lesbian and Gay Issues Into the Gerontology Curricula." Paper presented at the 18th annual meeting of the Association for Gerontology in Higher Education, Baltimore. *After demonstrating ways in which lesbian and gay voices have been marginalized within the field of gerontology, Will Hubbard offers strategies for including gay and lesbian issues in college and university gerontology courses.*

Hubbard, W.S. (1991). "A Career of Invisible Labor: Managing a Gay Identity in Gerontology." Unpublished manuscript. *Hubbard discusses the costs of heterosexism to researchers, educators, practitioners and the field of gerontology.*

Markowitz, L.M. (1991). "Homosexuality: Are We Still in the Dark?" ***Networker,* 15(1), 27-35.** *Laura Markowitz asks family therapists to evaluate their readiness to effectively serve gay and lesbian clients. She offers a comprehensive review of issues gay and lesbian clients often present to family therapists and makes intervention recommendations.*

Messing, A.E., Schoenberg, R. & Stephens, R.K. (1984). "Confronting Homophobia in Health Care Settings: Guidelines for Social Work Practice." In R. Schoenberg, R.S. Goldberg & D.A. Shore (Eds.) ***With Compassion Toward Some: Homosexuality and Social Work in America* (pp. 65-74). New York: Harrington Park Press. Also published in** ***Journal of Social Work and Human Sexuality,* 2(2/3), 1984.** *Alice Messing, Robert Schoenberg, and Richard Stevens discuss strategies for confronting and challenging heterosexism in health-care settings.*

Mohr, R.D. (1988). ***Gays/Justice: A Study of Ethics, Society, and Law.* New York: Columbia University Press.** *In chapter 12 (pp. 277-292), Richard Mohr offers a personal narrative describing his experiences while teaching a gay and lesbian studies course at a large university.*

Pharr, S. (1986). "Two Workshops on Homophobia." In K. Loebel (Ed.) *Naming the Violence: Speaking out About Lesbian Battering* (pp. 202-222). Seattle: Seal Press. *Suzanne Pharr gives step-by-step instructions for conducting workshops designed to counter homophobia.*

Raphael, S.M. (1980, October). "What Health Care Professionals Should Know About Older Lesbians." Paper presented at the annual meeting of the American Public Health Association, Detroit. Contact Sharon Raphael, California State University, Dominguez Hills, Department of Sociology, 100 E Victoria, Carson, CA 90747. *Based on the author's research (with Mina Meyer) among older lesbians, Sharon Raphael reviews dilemmas older lesbians face accessing health-care systems and offers intervention recommendations.*

Robinson (Meyer), M.K. (1980, October). "Support Systems for Older Lesbians." Paper presented at the annual meeting of the American Public Health Association, Detroit. Contact Mina Meyer at California State University, Dominguez Hills, Department of Sociology, 100 E Victoria, Carson, CA 90747. *With data from her research among older lesbians, Mina Robinson (Meyer) discusses ways in which older lesbians have been pro-active in forming their own systems of social support.*

Renzetti, C.M. (1989). "Building a Second Closet: Third Party Responses to Victims of Lesbian Partner Abuse." *Family Relations*, 38, 157-163. *Using questionnaire and in-depth interview data, Claire Renzetti reviews dimensions of violence in intimate lesbian relationships, and the effects on lesbians of helping professionals' unsupportive responses to requests for assistance. While Renzetti does not focus specifically on battering issues among older lesbians, her findings and intervention recommendations will be of interest to lesbians of all ages and to helping professionals called on to assist them.*

Roscoe, W. (1988). "Making History: The Challenge of Gay and Lesbian Studies." *Journal of Homosexuality,* **15(3/4), 1-40.** *Will Roscoe offers a critique of current models of teaching gay and lesbian studies and offers recommendations for improving the curricula.*

BOOKS

Blumenfeld, W.J. (Ed.) (1992). Homophobia: How We All Pay the Price. Boston: Beacon. *Warren Blumenfeld has compiled an accessible manual for confronting, challenging and overcoming heterosexism. Trainers will find his chapter on conducting anti-heterosexism workshops especially helpful.*

Corley, R. (1990). The Final Closet: The Gay Parents' Guide for Coming Out to Their Children. Miami: Editech Press. *Rip Corley, taking a clinical perspective, reviews the dilemmas commonly faced by gay and lesbian parents who choose to come out to their children and offers practical suggestions facilitating the coming out process.*

Dynes, W.R. (Ed.) (1990). *Encyclopedia of Homosexuality.* **New York: Garland Publishing.** *Wayne Dynes includes information on many pre-Stonewall era pioneering gay and lesbian liberation organizations.*

Gomez, J. (Ed.) (1984). *Demystifying Homosexuality: A Teaching Guide About Lesbians and Gay Men.* **New York: Irvington Publishers.** *Jose Gomez has compiled a comprehensive how-to resource guide for educators in gay and lesbian studies.*

Griffin, C.W., Wirth, M.J. & Wirth, A.G. (1986). *Beyond Acceptance: Parents of Lesbians and Gays Talk About Their Experiences.* **New York: St. Martin's Press.** *Carolyn Griffin, Marian Wirth, and Arthur Wirth effectively use the experiences of members of Parents and Friends of Lesbians and Gays to illustrate the costs of heterosexism on the individual, the family, and society.*

Harbeck, K.M. (1992). *Coming Out of the Classroom Closet: Gay and Lesbian Students, Teachers, and Curricula.* **New York: Harrington Park Press. Simultaneously issued as** *Journal of Homosexuality,* **22(3/4).** *Karen Harbeck's impressive collection of articles, reports of original research and essays will be of interest to educators/trainers attempting to integrate lesbian and gay issues into educational and practice settings.*

Hidalgo, H., Peterson, T.L. & Woodman, N.J. (Eds.) (1985). "Lesbian and Gay Issues: A Resource Manual for Social Workers." Silver Spring, Maryland: *National Association of Social Workers.* *This is a comprehensive collection of essays on social intervention issues and strategies.*

Kus, R.J. (Ed.) (1990). *Keys to Caring: Assisting Your Gay and Lesbian Clients.* **Boston: Alyson.** *Robert Kus offers an accessible collection of essays on various life concerns of gay and lesbian persons that will be of interest to educators and helping professionals.*

Island, D. & Letellier, P. (1991). *Men Who Beat the Men Who Love Them.* **New York: Harrington Park Press.** *David Island and Patrick Letellier discuss dimensions of domestic violence in gay male couple relationships and offer intervention recommendations.*

Mohr, R.D. (1988). *Gays/Justice: A Study of Ethics, Society, and Law*. New York: Columbia University Press. *Richard Mohr discusses implications of the ways in which gay men and lesbians are currently denied basic civil rights. A chapter on teaching a university-level gay and lesbian studies course will be of special interest to educators.*

Moses, A.E. & Hawkins, R.O. (Eds.) (1982). *Counseling Lesbian Women and Gay Men: A Life-Issues Approach*. St. Louis, Missouri: C.V. Mosby. *This is perhaps the best available source concerned with the provision of clinical and social services to gay and lesbian persons.*

Rochlin, M. (1992). "The Heterosexual Questionnaire." In M.S. Kimmel & M.A. Messner (Eds.) *Men's Lives* (second edition) (pp. 482-483). New York: Macmillan. Also published in *Changing Men*, Spring 1982. *The author provides a classic training tool for challenging heterosexist assumptions.*

Woodman, N.J. (1992) (Ed.). *Lesbian and Gay Lifestyles: A Guide for Counseling and Education*. New York: Irvington Publishers. *Natalie Woodman offers a comprehensive collection of articles focused on bringing gay and lesbian concerns into the center of social work education vision. Researchers will find Berger and Tully's gay and lesbian aging research review chapters helpful.*

Gay and Lesbian Outreach to Elders (GLOE) (1989). *Friendly Visitor Handbook*. San Francisco: Femedia III, Inc., 1622 Castro St., San Francisco, CA 94114. Alternate contact GLOE, 1853 Market St., San Francisco, CA 94103. *Grounded in the GLOE model of service delivery, this manual offers a how-to guide for preparing volunteers to work with older gay men and lesbians.*

Old Lesbian Organizing Committee (OLOC) (undated). *Facilitator's Handbook on Confronting Ageism for Lesbians 60 and Over*. Houston: OLOC (address listed under OLOC entry). *This feminist training resource focuses on deconstructing ageism. Educators attempting to include the voices of older lesbians in the design of training sessions on ageism will find this publication especially helpful.*

VIDEOS

Adair, P. (1978). *Word Is Out*. Available from Oscar Wilde Memorial Bookshop, 15 Christopher St., New York, NY 10014. *A landmark film in gay and lesbian studies, it includes visits with older gay and lesbian persons: Pat Bond, John Burnside, Elsa Gidlow, and Harry Hay.*

Gasper, M. (1991). *An Empty Bed*. Available from Lambda Rising, 1625 Connecticut Ave. NW, Washington, DC 20009, 800-621-6969. *A gay man in his sixties reflects on the challenges and triumphs of his life.*

Hamburger, L. (1992). *The Place I Call Home*. Contact Lisa J. Hamburger, c/o National Association for First Gerontology (NALGG), 1853 Market St., San Francisco, CA 94103. *This video visits the homes of gay and lesbian older adults, providing a multigenerational/cultural/socioeconomic look at housing issues that confront these men and women.*

Marshall, S. (1990). *Comrades in Arms*. Available from Filmakers Library, 124 E 40th St., New York, NY 10016. *Gay men and lesbians recall their experiences serving in the British Armed Forces during World War II.*

Muir, M. (1991) *West Coast Crones: A Glimpse into the Lives of Nine Old Lesbians*. Available from Wolfe Video,

PO Box 64, New Almaden, CA 95042. *From a feminist perspective, Madelaine Muir offers the experiences of nine old lesbians who have come together in a support group to define their own aging, challenge ageism, and celebrate being lesbian and old.*

Schiller, G. (1984). *Before Stonewall.* **Contact PBS Video, 1320 Braddock Pl. Alexandria, VA 22314.** *Narrated by Rita Mae Brown, Greta Shiller's video includes the testimonies of many older gay men and lesbians as it traces the historical development of today's liberated gay and lesbian communities.*

Snyder, P., Winer, L., Marks, H., and deKoenigsberg, P. (1984). *Silent Pioneers.* **Available from Filmakers Library, 123 E 40th St., New York, NY 10016.** *The film aired on some public television stations during gay and lesbian pride week in the mid-1980s. By offering glimpses into the lives of eight older gay men and lesbians, the film challenges stereotypes and myths concerning gay and lesbian aging and briefly discusses SAGE programming.*

Walton, P. (1991). *Out in Suburbia: The Stories of Eleven Lesbians.* **Available from Filmakers Library, 124 E 40th St., New York, NY 10016.** *This film aired on public television in the San Francisco Bay Area during gay and lesbian pride week in 1991. Walton offers a glimpse into the lives of lesbians who choose nonurban living. Three older lesbians are included in the video.*

Redi-Cassette-Go, 6253 Hollywood Bl. No. 818, Hollywood, CA 90028. *An entertainment company offering walk-in and mail-order sales of gay and lesbian-issue videos on a variety of topics. Order its catalog from the above address.*

PHOTOGRAPHS

Photographs of several older gay and lesbian persons, many of them active in GLOE programming, can be found in Cathy Cockrell's essay, "The Graying of the Gay Community," *San Francisco Sentinel*, 16(21) pp. 1,8-9,13.

Photographs of John Burnside and Harry Hay (pp. 231-247) and Elsa Gidlow (pp. 15-27) can be found in Nancy Adair and Casey Adair's *Word Is Out* (San Francisco: New Glide Publications, 1978).

Photographs of Paula Gunn Allen, Barbara Deming (in 1950), Elsa Gidlow, Monika Kehoe, Ida VSW Red,. and Jane Rule can be found in Margaret Cruikshank's *New Lesbian Writings* (San Francisco: Grey Fox Press, 1984).

Photographs of Barbara Deming (p. 58) and Mabel Hampton (p. 94) can be found in *Sinister Wisdom*, 43/44 (Summer).

A high-quality photograph of Monika Kehoe appears in Charlotte Painter and Pamela Valois's *Gifts of Age* (p. 99) (San Francisco: Chronicle Books, 1985).

Photographs of Barbara Macdonald (with partner Cynthia Rich, p. 193) and Elsa Gidlow (p. 16) can be found in J. Alexander, D. Berrow, L, Domitrovich, and M. Donnelly's *Women and Aging*. (Corvallis, Oregon: Calyx Books, 1986).

A photograph of Shevy Healey, older lesbian activist and writer, can be found in Amanda Bauer's article, "First U.S. Gay and Lesbian Conference on Aging Hits Homophobia/Ageism." *Aging Today*, 13(4), 1-2.

AUDIO CASSETTES

The American Society on Aging, in June of 1991, sponsored a conference on gay and lesbian aging, "Diversity With a Difference: Serving 3 Million Aging Gays and Lesbians." Audio tapes of eleven sessions that covered a wide range of topics are available from Conference Audio Services, 806 Lombard St., San Francisco, CA 94133.

GAY AND LESBIAN AGING
COLLEGE AND UNIVERSITY COURSES
CURRENTLY OFFERED

Those seeking to further explore gay and lesbian aging issues will find the listed classes of interest.

California State University, Dominguez Hills: Since the late 1970s Sharon Raphael has taught a course in lesbian and gay aging within the gerontology program at CSUDH. Contact Sharon Raphael, Ph.D., Department of Sociology, CSUDH, 100 E Victoria, Carson, CA 90747.

San Francisco State University: Since 1986 a course in gay and lesbian aging has been taught, first by Monika Kehoe and now by Sheryl Goldberg, in the gerontology programs at SFSU. Contact Sheryl Goldberg, The Institute on Gerontology, SFSU, 20 Tapia Dr., San Francisco, CA 94132.

San Francisco City College: Beginning in the spring of 1993, Margaret Cruikshank will teach a course entitled "Lesbian and Gay Aging Issues" under the auspices of CCFS's gay and lesbian studies department. Contact Margaret Cruikshank, Ph.D., CCSF, Box C256, 50 Phelan Dr., San Francisco, CA 94112.